# Panhandler Nation

## A Harm City Book

**Dust Cover**

When someone asks you for 'change' or a 'a dollar', as you cross the sidewalk, or flashes a 'will work for food' sign as you idle in your car at that busy intersection, what is really happening?

The big answer—according to urban survival writer James LaFond—is 'it depends'. And once you realize what that situation is dependent upon, well, then all the possible little answers can range from heartbreaking, to interesting, to terminally ugly.

Welcome to Panhandler Nation, otherwise known as the United States of America, the greatest debtor nation in history, ironically home to the most effective beggars imaginable.

Thank you Sir, your guilt is appreciated...

# Panhandler Nation

For more information about the author go to
jameslafond.com and click on the bio page

For Nadine, who gave a peanut butter and jelly sandwich to a man holding a 'will work for food' sign and had it smeared on her windshield.

## Contents

## Preface

I have a reputation for being hard on panhandlers. As a Darwinist I justify this callous disregard for my less fortunate fellows as expedient. For, among every ten legitimate downtrodden, brain damaged, woe befallen and deserving of my compassion fellow humans, lurks a violent criminal cloaking himself in the suffering of multitudes so that he can get one twitch closer to my wallet, and more importantly the throat that houses the oxygen feed, that powers the body, that transports that wallet and this brain around and about Harm City.

However, it would be wrong to say that I do not feel for these people. Indeed, on some days, they are the only human contact I have. Despite the fact that I identify with these people in all ways except for the abject shedding of their dignity, I shun them, for that could be me for want of a job and an archaic sense of defiance.

Upon consideration, what I most detest and most fear about panhandlers, is that they have become what society—what this materialist debtor identified in-group called America—yearns for them to be; plaintive guilt vectors submitting to the material order, and reaching like a flock of drowning souls for us to join them beneath the defiant horizon that separates us from total abject servitude.

When I walk by Crutch Boy twenty minutes from now on my way to purchase my groceries, a shiver of fear will trace the line of my spine—not because that could have been me, standing there open-hoped and soiled begging for the material expression of your suburban fucking whitebread guilt; but because that is *supposed* to be me, and the civilizing process will not have run its course in Our Town, until we are all on the cold street corner in our mind, praying for the Big Man to throw us someone else's crumbs.

When you see a panhandler on the corner tomorrow, don't get mad; don't get jealous; don't let your guilt kick into redistributive expression.

Remember that we have been conditioned to think that he is getting the things that we want without putting in the effort that we do, when he has in fact fallen for the ruse that is yet to consume us. When you drive by and shake your head, let it not be accompanied by the wish that you could get $300 dollars a day for holding a cardboard sign—for you could, if you were willing to sell your soul to The God of Things for that which will fit in your grimy paw.

Mourn him; the human that might have been, before he bought what your master is selling.

## Author's Notes

I have only a fraction of the contact with panhandlers that I had in the 1990s when I wrote my first set of violence books and when I formed my harsh opinions. Over the past three years I have recorded my notable interactions with the most plaintive urban souls I have encountered in Harm City on my website jameslafond.com. Consider that my prejudices were etched into me when I was gathering the material for the books the Fighting Edge, The Logic of Steel, The Logic of Force, and When You're Food.

If you would like to follow the ongoing exposition of woe that is postmodern urban life join me there at the website, and feel free to excoriate me for my foibles. I can only promise you one thing: that I will do my best to portray via the written word the subjects of my informal study in an accurate light and with an eye for their pain.

I am in many ways a primitive man; a man who believes in enemies. But my enemies, they are dear to me, for I am a ruthless lonely soul and they do define me.

### The Case for the Panhandler Genocide

## Why Beggars Should Starve

© 2012 James LaFond

I was headed through Baltimore City this morning to meet Charles and Josh for a training session over on the East Side. As is normally my practice, when confronted with a heap of ill-scented trash near the bus stop on Baltimore Street, I stepped over it. Imagine my irritation when the pile of trash sniveled, "Hey big guy, can you spare some change?"

I regarded the heap of refuse with disdain and declined, "No thanks man." and walked on. By the time I was well out of town, reading a book about a hard life lived by a real man, I had determined to take one more stab at panhandling as a self-defense concern.

# Panhandler Nation

This is not an attempt to earn a Tea Party endorsement for Republican Office. I dislike all panhandlers, particularly politicians. I am also not going out of my way to make this piece entertaining. This is a pure plea for sanity directed at the guilt-ridden with whom I share this hunting-matrix. I am just trying to protect our women and children through an appeal to clarity. My appeal is doomed. However, like the charity-giver that only gives to make his self feel better about the problem he cannot solve, I am likewise spitting into unforgiving winds for purely selfish reasons.

That nameless scumbag I stepped over, who has not a shred of remaining human dignity, may just be a beggar. My estimate is that two in every three panhandlers is a victim of society, parenting, genetics or all of the above, and could certainly use some help. I say let them starve. Let them huddle in the effusive gutters of our cities until they expire. Yes, here it goes, Crank Social Darwinist on parade.

In traditional societies these men would have been killed or enslaved by better men. The fact is a certain percentage of human males—reflected by the current homeless population—must be necessarily culled from any primitive population to insure a healthy dynamic society, capable of waging pitiless wars on its enemies. Unfortunately human society is no longer Genghis Khan compatible.

Why, you say, should we not tolerate these harmless men among us?

Because one out of every three homeless men are criminals! I love the guilty elite who built and fund Our Daily Bread in the upscale Mount Vernon area of Baltimore. The soup kitchen is two blocks from the Enoch Pratt Free Library. Because of this the library entrance is staffed like a Foreign Legion outpost by combative armed security guards. These guards are needed to keep the library safe— particularly the restrooms.

Men are usually aggressive. The losers, such as our homeless, are simply not good at aggression. They couldn't make it as athletes, backstabbing coworkers, soulless businessmen, obnoxious salesmen, or as military or law-enforcement personnel. However, that aggression is still latent within them, poorly contained by their diseased and drug-saturated minds, waiting to be stoked by envy or their basic human needs.

Here is the equation: your beggar is your son's pushy panhandler; your wife's strong-arm robber;

and your mother's terrifying toll-collector. The harmless beggars are not harmless because they lower our guard for the opportunistic panhandlers and condition our women and children to reach into their pockets and apologize as a first response to verbal aggression.

If I were Khan [even if just a middling not-so-great one] I would declare 20 lashes and a thousand dollar fine for the crime of giving to a beggar. For a second offense you would be impressed into service for six months clubbing baby seals in the Arctic. Before being permitted to rejoin civilization you would have to fight a convicted murderer in a cage on live TV. Your fine, the proceeds of your labor, and the purse for your fight would go to feed and house the homeless, who my warriors would have rounded up and herded onto my firing range; homeless no more, with their place in the sun to live out their brief yet productive lives.

Unfortunately, this equitable solution will not be coming to a planet near you anytime soon.

James LaFond, Sunday, 7/15/12

Man-Child Apocalypse & the Evils of Charity

**How to Combat Coercion Every Day of Your Life**

© 2012 James LaFond

**Boy Interrupted**

Last night, Friday, 10:23 PM, January 27th 2012, I
was making a purchase at a neighborhood grocery
store. I handed the young cashier a twenty and she
opened her drawer to make change. At that instant
a teenage boy approached me from behind pushing
a bicycle. The cashier looked at the boy nervously
as he nodded for me to get out of his way. I turned
to the girl, ignoring the boy, and extended my hand
for my change.

The girl did not move to make change but stood
staring alternately at myself and the boy in fear,
apparently of some kind of confrontation. At this
point the boy said, "I need to get by."

I ignored the rude lazy boy who would not apparently burn the additional calorie it would take to circle through the open lane behind me. The girl now stared at me in horror as if I had challenged the ruler of some barbaric nation in his very own domain. The boy then said, "I need to get by. Could you move?"

I said, "When I'm done here, I'll move."

Of course I could not complete my transaction because the cashier was still frozen in terror over the prospect of violence in her register lane, violence that she was cultivating through her submission to this boy's bullying, and her obvious wish that I would complaisantly do the same.

The boy, perhaps realizing that it seemed suspicious that he wanted to get between me and my money, and indeed get very close to an open drawer with hundreds of dollars in plain sight, finally made an attempt at tact, "Please, I just need to park my bike over there," as he pointed to the ice machine with his chin.

By now I was firmly in the 'rude zone' and ignored him, turning back to the cashier, and putting out my hand. The boy shook his head as if I were some

15

hopelessly daft person and wheeled his bike around to where it could have been a full minute before if he would not have insisted on interrupting my business.

The cashier looked at me in wide-eyed amazement, as if I had just given the class bully a wedgie before the entire student body. The boy, still far from being a man, even a young one, went about his business and so did I.

This episode points out three problems with modern American society:

1. That teenage boys [naturally] feel the need and the right to bully adults
2. That most adults—particularly women—live in fear of teenage boys, a fear that, rather than admit to, they cloak through an overweening desire to appease the little monsters and an insistence that men do likewise
3. That these two factors have resulted in a barbaric teenage substrata of our society that lives outside of the acceptable rules of behavior traditionally adhered to in **all previous** human societies, which has cultivated a sense of entitlement and

empowerment among teens which makes attacks on adults and isolated teens highly likely

## Boy Rewarded

A few weeks ago in the first week of January, on a Friday morning, in the same neighborhood, I boarded a bus packed with adults headed to work and youths headed to college. A high school student who was hooking school boarded the bus at the next stop and stood plaintively with hands out looking back toward the passengers. This drama is played out so often on buses, and has such a predictable outcome, that the bus driver just pulled off, knowing that the boy had hit the pity jackpot.

Three middle-aged women and one young woman all stepped forward to load this boy down with change, with statements such as, "There you go baby, something extra for lunch."

The boy did not even say thanks. He knew that he was entitled to this money. I will tell you this, if that boy steps up to a lone middle-aged woman at a bus stop at night, and she does not give him what he is entitled to, he will take it.

I have interviewed many such women, who have been mugged by the very boys that had begged change from me [panhandled] on the next stop up mere minutes before these women boarded the bus and said with a note of surprise, "I just got rolled by some kid!"

## Why Charity is Evil

Charity serves one purpose and one purpose only: to make the giver feel good about themselves. The nobility of medieval Europe admitted that this was the case, so intentionally took no steps to improve the lot of the poor. After all if there were no poor to beg than what opportunities would be left for the nobility to pave their way to heaven? Most Moslems were too far away to conveniently kill. There weren't enough intellectually inclined people to be labeled as heretics and hunted down in local crusades. And the Jews just seemed to be getting scarcer all the time. So, with so few readily available victims to be slain for God, charity was the default option into heaven.

Now, that might seem awful to you. But really, at least medieval man-butcher philanthropists were honest. Modern charity-givers would actually have us believe that they are doing it for those they give to; even espousing the cause of elevating the poor to their own level. The fact is people give to charity and to the punk skipping school and heading out to score some weed, for the same reason why good looking people like to have sex with the lights on, because it makes them feel good about themselves.

This modern combination of giving to the poor and also telling them that it is their right not to be poor, while making no demands on them, has cultivated a culture of intimidation. You see, ancient peasants knew that accepting charity confirmed their inferior status. The bums of the modern world know no such thing.

As a Darwinist, with full knowledge that charity is evil and that giving is nothing more than an attempt by the giver to either find comfort in submitting to mild aggression or feel good about giving, I accept that all who are willing to so give and so submit deserve to be preyed upon. These heaven-bound people have self-selected themselves as prey items on the earthly social menu. I suppose martyrdom, even of this anemic variety, does have its appeal.

Just remember that if you have decided to play such a minor league martyr than you have consigned some of those who are weaker than yourself to intimidation and the entire spectrum of violent crime that grows in its fertile soil.

## How Civility Cultivates Victims

A commitment to civility in the classic sense is a bad thing unless the people committed to this sense of civility—of avoiding confrontation and not being rude—adhere to the code of the duel.

Yes, I just wrote that, and I mean it.

You see, we have inherited our sense of civility from generations of extinct European whack jobs who would engage in a lethal duel at the mere hint of an insult. Adhering to such a strict code of civility in a society where it is not acceptable for me to cane Bike Boy, with full knowledge that I would then be called upon to defend the righteousness of my actions in a duel to the death against his older brother, makes rudeness inherently powerful. In all three of the situations outlined above [including the lone woman against the panhandling punk] the person who is most committed to the rude course of action has the upper hand up until the actual commencement of physical hostilities.

In modern self-defense situations the rude party usually possesses the strategic advantage and hence *position* [angle-of-attack] and *initiative*. Holding the superior *position* and the *initiative* typically translates to a *tactical advantage*. This process is called *momentum* and is one reason why almost all violent crime is successful.

**Never Give In**

Although I am not recommending being loud, offensive, derisive or insulting, and certainly not threatening, if we actual want to retard the predatory development of the American Man-child, then we should always say no to their rude demands. These punks and the adult beggars that proceeded them on the social scene at busy intersections back in the God-forsaken eighties have unwittingly trained multiple generations of Americans to step out of their way and/or immediately begin digging into their pockets, wallets or purses as a first response to verbal aggression.

If you are that guy who would have stepped aside for Bike Boy, or that gal who was willing to open her purse for Bus Boy, than you are already a highly trained mugging victim.

At least you are good at something.

James LaFond, January 28th 2012

### Harm City Holdout

## A Normal Saturday Night in Baltimore

© 2012 James LaFond

## Last of the White Savages

I have been called hyperbolic for suggesting Baltimore is an exceptionally dangerous place. I have also been called a 'scary person' and a 'badass' for having survived three decades on foot, at night, in this mid-sized city that has managed to remain in the top ten for most violent American cities every year since the early nineties. I disagree with both of these characterizations. I might be a 'weirdo', an 'eccentric', a 'Bohemian'. But I am no badass and I have not inflated Baltimore's violent nature. I do have 'bad hips' in jiu jitsu parlance, and that could be loosely translated as me being a badass. And, yes, I have focused some measure of negative attention on my hometown. But that is about the extent of my 'street cred'.

For decades I was just a hard-working scrub that did not make much money, and was stuck in the city that my more lucratively living relatives managed to flee from. My wife and I had decided to forgo a two-income suburban home so that she could actually raise our children as opposed to that being accomplished by a daycare center. Now that my sons are adults, living suburban lives, I have 'opted out' of the 'rat race', and rent a room in the city, so that I can pursue my writing. The subjects I write about are not lucrative so I have stayed behind, a white trash loner in a majority black city overrun with gang sets and group-based crime, though it is undergoing a minor renaissance in select areas.

The violence study I did in the late 90s is skewed in a number of ways. For instance I did not seek interviews with strange women out of respect for them: "Excuse me miss, I am the Violence Guy. I would like to know if you have been raped lately; does your husband beat you..."

The survey was however, comprehensive to my life-way and the lives of those I know, and the men I sought out in my quest to widen and deepen my understanding of my environment—just one singular environment out of hundreds of urban centers across this continent. Let us say then that The Violence Project did generate an accurate 'urban working class violence profile', with the understanding that the female victim numbers are both skewed and weak, and that the cultural setting is regionally distinct and the population density moderate.

The process of collecting the information and turning it into thematic books was made more dynamic, more interesting, by the fact that I worked at night in various locations, all of which necessitated me travelling through some of the worst parts of Baltimore at the worst times. I have always worked in supermarkets, usually on the night crew. Night crew clerks make their best money on Saturday night, when they get paid overtime. When I was writing my violence books I had at least one crazy incident or threat a week; providing plenty of timely illustrations to help illuminate those other people's misadventures that I had studied. It might come as no surprise to learn that much of that 'crazy' stuff [I'll ballpark it and say 30%] happened on Saturday nights.

Inspired by Robert Wagner, homeowner advocate and infomercial humanitarian, I am now living in 'reverse-retirement'. I no longer prostitute myself

for Saturday night OT, but stay home and write.
Last night, Saturday, December 16th, 2012, I agreed
to do my boss a favor and work for a man who is on
vacation. What I am about to relate to you is simply
a trip from Northeast Baltimore to Eastern
Baltimore County. I used to take such commutes
360 days per year from 1992 through 2006. The
story I am about to tell you, is being told, not
because I rate it as crazy or unusual; but because it
represents my typical work commute through the
late 1990s and early 2000s. I am now looking at
things from an older, more enlightened perspective,
in a city that has been somewhat altered for better
and for worse.

Early on last night I decided to pay special attention
to as many facets of nocturnal Harm City life as
possible. I also, did not take any written notes.
When you are out there with a notepad, everyone
treats you differently, mostly more deferentially
than otherwise. [I do believe that this went some
ways toward inoculating me from violence back
when I was 'The Violence Guy'.] So, I write this
today from memory; a micro-memoir, a slice of life
from the perspective of one of America's most
reviled organisms: the stay-behind white-trash
urban survivor; a being with no egalitarian social

traction; a low-caste semi-person with no wealth or privilege inherited from the 'master race' that wiped out the red man and enslaved the black man; and also a man with no excuses for his failure to materially thrive...

**The Peace Pipe**

10:45 p.m.

I would be taking the downtown bus and then an out-of-town bus, to get to the East Side. Cross-town bus service was finished for the night and a cab lift would cost me $40. I walked a half mile to Harford Road in Hamilton, the last neighborhood south of Parkville. Parkville is a very large zip code that straddles the city/county line. Lately the crime has been much worse in Parkville than in Hamilton. The wave of Section Eight subsidized welfare mothers and their criminal spawn has migrated through Hamilton and is no besieging my betters up the road. The night is completely overcast and moist, a slight drizzle in the upper air, dissipating to a foggy mist at street level. I do not pass a soul on this secondary street.

When I arrive at Harford Road city cop cars are racing out to Parkville where the county police chopper can be heard hovering two miles to the north. Two Saturday nights past [2:30 AM Sunday] there was a double fatal stabbing out there, so that crosses my mind as I cross the street. I also wonder about Will up at the 7-11 just south of the county line. He's been robbed a few times this year and twice had to lock up the store when county cops drove rioters from the VFW hall down into the city. I wonder if perhaps all of these city cops are headed out to repay the favor by driving some Harm City Hood Rats north into Whitebreadistan...

**10:55 p.m.**

I take up a position by the curb at the bus stop across from an old church and notice a small crowd of teenagers up the street on the other side. I look down the street and see a few bar patrons coming and going at the local dive. One of them comes north and walks by me, speaking to someone on her cell phone. I should have been minding my Six O'clock but I was minding hers. She was in her mid-twenties, 5' 1", 115 pounds, with b-cups, long, thick, silky black hair, a long thin nose, and a nice...a, voice—that's right I was attracted to her melodic tone. I can recall no other features; have not even the slightest inkling as to the anatomical properties that might have been responsible for stretching that long tight white sweater over her new snug blue jeans.

I immediately began looking for a man. Women this good looking, particularly the rare good-looking white woman of Baltimore, do not travel alone. She is either a vice cop who will try to chat me up; or she has just had a fight with her drunk boyfriend. Sure enough, I hear her confirming 'suspicion two' as she walks past me toward the crowd up the street, "No, no baby, I don't go with him anymore. Oh, he's back down at the bar. I'm not getting back with him..."

And so she strolled on by, appealing to the conscience of some poor sap that she had obviously dumped some time ago, trying to get him to toss the remote aside and get in his reason for her calling so he can come pick her up and then kick himself in the mind when she kisses him on the cheek and heads into mom's house with that 'sorry for the lack of chemistry' look on her face...

**11:00 p.m.**

Being a man of science I observed this young lady's progress up the sidewalk under the street lights, placing her BMI at...let me see...darn I forgot my calipers—at about, just right. Look, I'm a boxing coach; body-typing is my business I will have you know. Just as she passed the next stop, she headed back my way, pocketing her phone. She was being pushed south by the group of screaming and laughing kids. She picked up her step until she got down to my stop, and then began lurking behind me, no longer on the phone, just pacing nervously. The kids kept coming down this side of the street having crossed 150 yards north of my position.

The group was 14-15 years old and middle class. These are often the most obnoxious youngsters, because they are not real hoodlums, but want that same level of respect, so tend to be real loud. There were four males and two females. This is a ratio that will generally insure foolish behavior on the part of at least one of the males, as he tries to show off for the girls. The woman was now milling around the stop, having suddenly found a use for the grungy looking old dude in the bomber jacket, hooded black sweatshirt, torn painter's pants, Polygamy Porter hat, and shredded work boots.

As the kids neared us they got quiet, all stared at me, and then surrounded me. The lady then darted for the wall of the building behind the bench and between two bushes.

'Good girl' I thought as I palmed my Bic pen in my right coat pocket.

I had a welterweight in the street behind me, a middleweight and a featherweight over my left shoulder. Between me and the dark-haired girl with the nice pale skin was a lightweight in a windbreaker and ski cap and a female. To my right was the other female. My right foot was on the curb and my hands were in my pockets.

A moment of silence while some punk grows a set of hopeful balls...

In situations like this I kind of get tantric. I focus on one antagonist and do not take my eyes from him as I visualize doing the same thing to him over and over and over again. I pick that option out of my limited physical inventory without thinking about it. I just go with my emotional state. If I'm alert and feeling sharp I just visualize checking, gouging and sprawling. If I'm angry I visualize punching and stomping. If I'm feeling sluggish I visualize stabbing.

I was feeling really sluggish. By the time he began talking to me I had already stabbed him in the throat repeatedly in my mind. My right hand was wrapped around my plastic ink pen, and my left hand was open, ready to slide out of my coat pocket and palm his right shoulder so I could pull him into the stab.

He said, "Yo, yo got a menthol cigarette?"

I looked through him; not a stare-down, or a glare, just a vacant look.

## A Ghetto Context Break...

*First, let's make one thing crystal clear: when a male in Baltimore asks a strange man on the street for a smoke, it is not about the cigarette. The purpose is 1. intimidation, 2. bonding, or 3. the beginning of 'an interview' which will determine your suitability as a victim. Since I am not psychic I always assume 3. to be the case.*

*In Baltimore two kinds of smokers smoke menthols: blacks and white stoners. White drunks smoke Camels, Winstons, Cowboy Killers, etc. This kid actually began on a diplomatic note. We can forgive him for not realizing that he had the ill luck to run into the only working class white Baltimorean who does not smoke and get high. This was the equivalent of Daniel Boone taking Rebecca on a trek, and, upon passing a Mingo drifter on the trail, suggesting they smoke a peace pipe. He might as well have said to the girl closest to him, "Hey baby, I know how to talk to these old fiends."*

**Back to Our Hip-hop Hero**

He kept looking at me but stepped back a little, just out of arm's reach, "Yo, can I have a menthol cigarette?"

I looked through him, feeling myself empty out, draining myself of thought and emotion as I, in my mind's eye, trapped and stabbed, trapped and stabbed, trapped and stabbed.

Now, when I begin visualizing an action when confronted my 'go cue' is touch-approach-deploy. I will—if alone and not protecting a non combatant—never act without being touched, charged, chased, followed, or having a weapon deployed against me. This is not ideal. Once I have brainwashed myself to react in a certain way I will stick with that until there is separation or until I am touched again. If I get touched again that is what I call my 'devolution cue'; I just become an animal. My frame-of-mind may be described like so: I've turned myself into a bullet and loaded myself into their gun. They can shoot themselves or put the gun down.

I don't know how ethical you think that is. I am not a gregarious person, not a talker. I am also not a dominating personality, not a yeller. I'm a quiet private little person who draws a line in his mind and waits for it to be crossed. So, my method of mentally cuing up for such encounters suits me. If I was a coked up offensive lineman maybe yelling would be the way to go.

They were all standing still. This guy was not going to initiate. I expected the touch to come from behind, and kept visualizing launching on this guy when that happened. If an adult male gets attacked he needs to get visibly marked up and mark up as many of the 'innocent' youths as possible, to take them out of the witness pool.

I am not afraid of these guys, but of the police, the state's attorney; the people who will take my freedom away for having the indecency to defend myself in their domain.

He then screeched as he did a close kneel with hands on knees like a transvestite imitating Marilyn Monroe singing to JFK, "Please give me a menthol cigarette!"

I kept staring and visualizing as he repeated this same plea the same way over and over and over again, literally screaming at the top of his lungs for a 'menthol cigarette'.

Then, the girl next to him, off my right shoulder, reached over to him and slapped him in the shoulder with her fingertips, "Fool, don't you see he ain't playin'!"

For emphasis she pointed with her other hand to my hands in my front coat pockets. The boy then stepped back and looked around at his friends as I continued to visualize and stare.

He barked, "Yo, whateva whateva. Lez head down da street yo."

With that they were off down into the center of Hamilton to do whatever important things remained to be done. The brunette then walked up to my left shoulder, "Hey sweetie, could you spare a cigarette?"

She was streetwise enough to know that this encounter had nothing to do with cigarettes. I looked down into her pretty brown eyes and said, "Actually miss, I don't smoke, I really don't."

She said, "Wow, have a nice night baby", and walked back up the street as she slid her phone out of her back pocket, past two guys in their early twenties who had just crossed the street and were noting that the cops had returned from Parkville already. That is when my bus rolled up.

## Strange Ways

11:35 p.m.-1:00 a.m.

10-15 years ago the #19 bus would have held, not only the five working passengers commuting home, but a gang set as well. It seems the Harford Road Boyz have gone the way of Rome and I caught a nap as the other patrons texted, facebooked and nodded off. I used to pass through downtown daily. Now it is quarterly. My transfer point was on Baltimore Street, known as 'The Block' where the strip clubs are. When I was younger this area would be overrun by groups of suburban 21-year-olds and creepy old perverts, with a sprinkling of hookers.

I found The Block was much changed. There was a heavy police presence. Baltimore has recently garnered some gay pride and formula racing tourist dollars, and is trying to overcome the bad image cast by HBO miniseries and 2012's Saint Patrick's Day flash mob attacks on tourists [See Stoning Baboons].

There is, ominously, only one hooker, and she is very good looking with her pimp maintaining a high profile. I saw a handful of white couples, paired up in fours. I saw about ten other white male pedestrians in pairs and alone. I estimated about 500 black male pedestrians, mostly in groups of three to six, and a handful of Hispanics.

There was about a dozen of us people of mixed age, but mostly older, waiting at the stop, observing the insanity around us. I spotted about 30 black women, travelling in pairs and trios. The crazy thing was, these were largely West Baltimore ghetto girls who had dressed up in almost nothing, seemingly in competition with the unseen dancers, in order to pick up men. None of them were comfortable in their high heels, and I would say that the average size was 5'9" 200 lbs. The clingy miniskirts were so short that any normal step would render them naked from the waist down.

There were three people working drug packages and one guy eating discarded pizza crust off the sidewalk while he tried to sell discarded bus tickets.

The white men that were visible were all driving; either cop cars or luxury sedans and SUVs. One SUV-load of stoned and drunk white men were shadowing a group of three black girls, calling out the window asking about prices, assuming they were hookers. A young guy standing at the stop next to me yelled to the insane looking Eastern European drunk that was hanging out the window, "Yo fool, they either givin' it away or kickin' yo ass. Nobody pays fo pussy anymore up in dis joint."

Our next laugh came as two women, escorted by a single submissive man, argued violently as they walked the two blocks in our view along Baltimore. It took these girls from 12:05 to 12:30 to cover two blocks, only to kick off their high heels and begin punching each other.

The 11:30 p.m. bus had not come.

The 12:00 a.m. bus did not come.

The 12:30 a.m. bus did not come.

The two old ladies with their canes were looking beat as the rain began rolling in.

The 1:00 a.m. bus did not come.

Then the cops started shutting down the intersections with traffic cones and I left my co-commuters behind and walked west two blocks.

1:10 a.m.

There was no bus in sight and cabs were getting scarce. Two gorgeous after-hours dancers and their body guards were dismounting from an Escalade and headed down toward the Hustler Club and the other fleshpots.


**Beam Me Up, Haji**

A Middle Eastern dude banked his cab around off of Light Street. I waived him over and he passed me by, headed into the block to pick up some drunks, who were far better dressed. Then he noticed the cones and backed up, asking me where I was going.

He was all ears when he found out I was in need of a $60 fare. As we rolled through the Inner Harbor and out the East Side we traversed what was effectively a deserted wilderness. We passed two traffic stops and an arrest in progress by the city cops, and one traffic stop and an arrest in progress by the county cops.

I like how cabbies, mostly recent immigrants, really try to provide the best in customer service by dialing in a radio station that they guess will please their patron. He switched the hip-hop to country, then to classic rock, then—took a good look at me— and switched on an AM channel for a book interview. I never stopped looking out the window during this process. When he had tuned in the talk show I smiled, and he finally spoke, "Good evening to you sir."

I said, "Thanks for the lift Sir, I really appreciate it."

But I thought to myself, 'Why can't half of the people in Baltimore be as decent as this guy?'

So there you have it, a typical Saturday night in Harm City from the lone pedestrian viewpoint. Put it together with the epilogue below and you have nearly a week of fairly usual encounters. In addition, according to my supervisor, my exposure to violence is about to shift by an order of magnitude, back to where it was in the 90s. The store had been open 24 hours before, but sustained so much crime—including shootings, stabbings and bodies flying through the front window—that business hours had been scaled back. We are poised to climb back on the crazy train in two weeks, which should be to the material benefit of this column.

## I a Killa!

After outlining this article on Sunday morning I was unable to complete it until today. I am glad it happened this way. You see, upon realizing that any 'civilized' readers would think me odd or wrong for staring at a man or youth demanding a cigarette instead of engaging him in polite conversation and the denial of the habit, I decided to break a 15 year policy, and say "I don't smoke", politely to the next man or youth to ask me for a cigarette.

As fate would have it he was waiting for me at 11:43 p.m., Wednesday night, December 19th, two days before the end of the world. I turned the corner to the suburban market where I work and two gutter zombies were scrounging for used butts to smoke. The big white trash guy looked me over and decided I was not to be harassed. The small black man, about my size, was, however, drunk. Normally a guy his age, in his early 30s, will know right off the bat when he sees one of those rare white men who are not terrified of black men. He was off his game.

As I walked toward him he said, "Hey brutha can you spare a smoke?"

I responded politely, this being one of my benefactor's customers, "I don't smoke."

He became aggressive, "Don' lie; you be lyin'!"

As I passed him I said, "We can discuss that." I drew my razor and butted it against my hip to expose the edge. Before he had even turned around and saw that I was armed he was chanting, "I kill people yo! You be lyin ta a stone-cole killa!"

I got to the door and turned to face him. His threats continued as he retreated, "I be killin' people—I be commin' fo ya yo!"

He never did see the blade as I kept it hidden. That use of a weapon is called 'holding', and, despite the beliefs of self-defense instructors and law enforcement, it is common.

As my supervisor let me in I laughed, "Can you believe that maggot wants to kill me for not smoking?"

He responded, "He'll get his chance in two weeks when we start staying open all night."

Of course, this man was not threatening me because I did not smoke. He was just using smoking as a point of departure for his violent art; his decent into the dominant chest-thumping of the Urban American Male of African descent who, thanks to our centuries-old corrupt slave mentality, believes himself to be a genetically superior combatant. And why shouldn't he? He lives in a society of white cowards, most of who would stand by shivering as soon as he declared his superiority.

I don't blame him for failing to realize that he had come across one of those nearly extinct white apes that does not care to bow to his dark master. I blame the generations of soft she-males of European descent, the same people that told me in the 1970s that white men weren't tough enough to box; that told me in the eighties that I could never hope to kick-box with an Asian; that told me in the 90s that non-Hispanic men were not fit to stick-fight; the same soft society that tells me now that I am too old and not Mexican enough for manual labor, even as I work circles around men less than half my age.

I don't blame the righteous tobacco-craving representative of the Urban Master Race. I blame the sniveling society that spawned him; the society whose members cannot face the sunrise without caffeine; noon without nicotine; and sundown without alcohol.

You see I am not a 'badass' just a knucklehead who refuses to acknowledge any master but the man who pays me and the government he serves.

## Two Rearguard Actions against the Subhuman Hordes

© 2013 James LaFond

This is not my first Darwinian rant against the bums of the New World Order [See The Case for the Panhandler Genocide], and it is not my last. These creatures have been becoming more virulent and better organized, and are now the enemy in an undeclared culture war in our cities. Somehow the entitlement mentality cultivated by our society since my birth in the early 1960s [Perhaps I am the Antichrist like that hillbilly preacher said?] has finally produced a generation of aggressively violent bums.

In the past they only became dangerous when they were about to die from exposure. Now they organize as a matter of course, and even have contingency plans for dealing with the cops. Panhandler Nation will be my ongoing chronicle of their victories and defeats. As indicated by the subtitle above, I do not recognize their humanity. I must treat them as human under the laws enforced by my sniveling masters. But I cannot be forced to regard them as spiritually, ethically, or morally human. I remain free in mind at least.

## Zombie Winter

It is winter; time for beggars to band together into packs and go on the offensive. I remember one winter night when it was 18 below in the late 1990s. I got off the #19 bus downtown at around 11:00 PM. Three bums were huddled over the steam grates trying to keep warm. One, an old bent one, looked up at me, walking by in my overcoat, and croaked, "Coat, coat!"

He walked toward me with arms outstretched, as if he were a zombie wanting to feast on my brains. His two friends joined him, limping and shuffling after me, as I picked up my pace and left them behind. I sincerely hope they died of exposure on that wintry night. If they did—they must surely be in the ground by now, fifteen years on—they have certainly been replaced by other noxious beings, now populating our gutters with fresher DNA.

I recall the bum stompings of that time, how teenagers were stomping these guys out and crippling them for fun. I thought that was disgusting, but was glad that more bums had been crippled. These are the fiends that will pounce on me ghoul-like if I ever fall ill or injured on the winter streets of Baltimore. Whether they are the sore-covered white heroin addicts or the ashen-hued black alcohol-zombies, they are the jackals of the urban night, ready to strip the very clothes from your back. I hope more of them freeze on this 15-degree January day, and into what promises to be an even colder night.

Oh, I have a request: if any Harm City reader ever encounters a Latino or Asian panhandler, please fill us in using the comment section below. So far, according to my experience, it seems to be a white and black thing.

**Martha**

Martha is a 65-year-old grandmother. She has lived in the same neighborhood for her entire life. About

48

15-years ago the crack and heroin epidemic washed over her neighborhood. So, as of 1998, she could no longer walk to the store. Since then she has driven the five blocks to her local market. Unfortunately, since dealers have recently evolved to using cars to supply their clients, as opposed to working corners 'open air' style, once she gets to the local market, it is no longer safe to get out of the car. She shops with her adult son, a self-described vigilante, who has attacked street people before. She pulls up in the loading zone and he goes into shop, unafraid of the gathering scum, demanding cigarettes and cash.

Martha will roll down her window and give money to harmless seeming bums, dispensing perhaps $50 per a year in this manner, despite her son's disapproval. She claims to have good instincts, and has noted that more and more of these panhandlers seem dangerous or 'no good' and has been declining to roll down her window and dispense money.

The reason for this is that drug dealers who work from cars use busy retail lots to ply their trade to obscure their business. I have interviewed the owner of this market, who has informed me that the storefront and parking lot are a 'free-fire zone' as far as they are concerned. This retailer will only commit to protecting customers when they are inside the store, out of fear that any attempt to protect customers on the store front or lot will be an admission of liability and open them up to law suits. They will call the police, but discourage employees from offering themselves as witnesses.

The two local cops I have interviewed about this have told me that they are loath to enforce misdemeanors on the property of any business owner with this attitude, and have specifically pointed out this retailer as a problem location because of their encouragement of illegal cabbies, or 'hacks'.

Last week Martha was waiting for her son to come out of the store when an apparently insane panhandler approached her with a gas can. She was nice to him. After hassling her for a while, and threatening her with the nozzle of the gas can, he went on his way. Then she noticed that he had an 80-year-old woman pinned in her car. Martha called the store, and got an assurance that they would call the cops. She then rolled down her window and asked the creep to leave the old lady alone. The creep disappeared as his crew swooped in to take over the operation.

You see, these lots are now worked by organized crews—against whom no lone legitimate old-style bum stands a chance of holding his territory—who divide labor between the panhandler, the mouth, and the muscle. Gascan was working with 300-pound Junky Joe with his 120-pound brindle attack dog; a 350-pound 'side-kick', and a crack ho. A crew like this works together with lookouts and muscle and relief mouth to score $40. When they score their $40 the car-mobile dealer will cruise in and sell them their four hits of whatever they are using to kill themselves.

The crack ho began a confrontation with Martha, which got ugly, and drew Martha out into an argument; where, she would have just avoided a confrontation with one of the men. The entire point was to have two women arguing when the cops rolled up so that Gascan would be all but forgotten, already working the next lot, and Junky Joe just an innocent witness. The cops only buy so much of this bullshit, but it muddies the waters enough to make sure there is no citation or arrest.

Junky Joe had already intimidated the parcel pickup clerk into not giving a statement. The security guard hid inside and peeked out the window from under the banana sign. Martha had asked the store to call the cops so that her son would not get arrested for fighting Junky Joe and his cohorts. Again, you see the separation of job responsibilities, common to a criminal organization, even of the lowest order. If Junky Joe had to fight Martha's son he had a dog and an accomplice to stack the odds, and his crack ho witness to even the odds in court.

The cops just took statements and made sure Martha got off the lot. She does not know if they made Junky Joe leave.


**A Rough Dude**

This story is second-hand and out-of-state but comes from a good source. The tale is set in the small brownstone ghetto city of Newburgh in New York, not far from Westpoint in the Hudson Valley, sprawling around a state prison. This formally middle class city is now inhabited by many of the loved-ones and offspring of the prison inmates.

A contractor, who has his own small construction business stopped into a neighborhood market to get cigarettes and refreshments. When he stepped away from the counter a young teenager asked him for a cigarette. Of course, this is never about the cigarette!

The man responded that he did not have a cigarette.

The teen became combative, claiming to have seen the man purchase cigarettes, and demanding one.

The man threatened the teen.

The teen deployed a hatchet!

The man told the teen that he would take the hatchet and forcibly place it in a specific bodily cavity.

The teen's mother appeared and threatened the man.

The man, 'a rough dude', threatened them both.

The mother dashed upstairs to her apartment as the teen opened up his cell phone and called in the troops.

The store owner told the man that he best leave, because the kid was well-connected in the area.

The mother came downstairs with a bowl of bleach and threw it at the man's face. The contractor had fortunately pulled away in time to save his eyes, but not his coat, which was ruined.

The man went out to his truck, got in, and pulled off. As he was pulling off an armed gang of mixed-age males was converging on the store.

This is a bare-bones second-hand account, but it is very recent, from just last week, and illustrates well why Martha was approached by a panhandler who had such heavy backup. This is a war, if of the lowest order, and the panhandlers are winning. If you are not a bum, and live in a mid-sized East Cast city, you are living in occupied territory, behind enemy lines.

Whether you are Grandma Martha or 'a rough dude', be careful.

## Grandma

If you are Grandma, look out.

The first indication that you are being targeted for crime is that you are approached by a man that you do not know. They are always criminals and are always no good.

Secondly, our society is now so corrupt, that youth is not a good indicator of criminal capacity. All of those criminal youths from the 70s, 80s and 90s did not—unfortunately—get killed. Most of them just got older and uglier, not any better. Below is an excellent example from this past Sunday the 20th of January 2013.

One Sunday a month I spend with my mother in her suburban enclave. This past Sunday we went for a walk before the game came on TV. She pointed out a group of teenagers out clowning around and said that she was worried about there being so many in the area. I assured her that they were all addicted to alcohol and numerous illegal drugs, which they could easily afford thanks to their parents' affluence, and should not be much of a threat. They just want to get high and goof off. As we discussed this two men in their late twenties or early thirties approached us. I stepped behind her so that they could pass. They kept coming two abreast and she stepped off the sidewalk into the mud!

My mother is over 70 and we now have upper class adult men who think she should step aside for them, and she is fine with that, because we are all supposedly one gender now. I told her that it was unacceptable and she just did not get it, and I am sure, would have been horrified to know what I was thinking. You see, she does have a sense that her benighted suburban paradise is going bad. She is just looking in the place that the newspapers have told her to look for trouble. [Junky Joe and his crew, and the mother of Hatchet Boy, were all in their 30s, and those events generated no arrests, will never become factors in the law-enforcement database, or the world as seen through newspapers and news programs.] The surest sign that you are living in a predatory culture is incivility to the elderly and the weak.

That piece-of-gay-ass that thought it was fine for an old lady to walk in the mud so he could prance along in his slippers is probably not a criminal. But, if one of those teens that she pointed out were to give her trouble, I guarantee you that that sissy in his bedroom slippers, and his boy-toy that sashayed beside him, would stand idly by. In a civil society it would have been legal and even commendable for me to whip both of those queers for disrespecting my mother. But in our world, it would be a crime, so

I did not ruin her game-day with the spectacle of her son, a grandfather himself, committing a crime.

**The problem is that we live in a society where it is increasingly unacceptable to be a man. And without men all you have is animals and their prey.**

Little Eddie Horn: Wonderboy of Beggars

© 2013 James LaFond

I hate panhandlers. However, I have known the occasional likeable panhandler. These are really the most tragic cases. Because any person capable of shinning as a panhandler, you sense instinctively, could have done really well at something more acceptable. They might be my enemies, but that does not mean their job is easy. As you might suspect the likeable panhandler is a versatile person; something more than a rack to hang a cardboard sign on.

**Eddie and The Man**

I had been managing a ghetto supermarket for two years now and the applications were flooding in: the more men you fire, the more want to work for you; that is the counterintuitive truth. A regular source of applicants was a men's halfway house a mile down the street. A boy, it seemed, was waiting for me by the courtesy counter. He smiled and waved, holding up an application. I motioned that I would be right there and went behind the counter to confer with Silenshay, a cute mathematics major, who wanted to speak with me.

The boy was stretching on his tiptoes trying to get a look at our conversation so my beautiful assistant, escorted me Bob Barker like up into the officer. There was a conspiratorial tone to her voice, as she once again made ever pretext imaginable to touch me and I shuffled back nervously trying to keep my bank account out of her gunsights, "Mister Jimmy, that fool boy is trouble. Mister Duz caught him shoplifting last year—and look at this."

She then held up a forged Selective Service registration form that this fellow was trying to pass off as his I.D., "Look at where he changed the age Mister Jimmy. We told him you were busy—besides I don't like the way he looks at me."

"In that case Silenshay, I think I'll hire him to replace me."

She snorted—and somehow made it sound cute, "You don't mean that Mister Jimmy."

I took the I.D. to the copier, made a copy for my records, and attempted to pass my highly professional assistant in the hallway, who stood with one hand on her jutting hip as the last two buttons on her blouse attempted heroically to contain what she had somehow jammed into the undersized garment, "Mister Jimmy, what am I going to do about this?"

I faked left and darted right as I advised, "I'm sure NASA has worked something out."

I ran downstairs and emerged into the area before the courtesy to parlay with the young man, who had provided I.D. indicating that his name was Eddie Horn. To my dismay he was arguing with Mymecca, my big no-nonsense courtesy clerk, who was wagging her finger at him and calling him 'boy'.

He was pacing angrily as I approached him with his I.D., "Nice documentation Eddie—hey, I can't have you cussing my girls. You have to go."

He seemed relieved to be talking to me, "I'm sorry Mister Jimmy. It's just that I admire you so much; just want to be one of the men on your crew, and it seems like everywhere I go, there is some lady with a gigantic ass wagging her finger at me and telling me what to do."

I put my arm around him and walked him toward the door, "Look Eddie you are welcome back to update your application and to shop, but you have to respect my employees, particularly the women."

"I know Mister Jimmy. But why do they get to be in charge. Why do I have to respect women when they don't respect me?"

I stopped and nodded at the registers, "You see all of those things, they bring in the money; and the girls, even the ones with the gigantic asses and wagging fingers, they operate them for me. Eddie, I can't even operate this cell phone. All of these chicks they run this place. I just make sure everybody follows the rules and feels safe. Any man that comes in here and talks disrespectfully to the ladies has to go. It's an implicit social contract. I do that for them, and they let me pretend to be in charge of all this stuff."

A deep, previously un-guessed revelation, seem to wash over Eddie's dark brown eyes. He had an 'aghast' expression on his face as he looked out over the parking lot, and then turned to look at me with something approaching pity, "Wow Mister Jimmy. So even if I get to be the boss—even if I get to be you—there is still going to be some giant-assed lady bossing me?"

"Eddie, wherever we go, whatever we do, some chick is going to be telling us what to do."

Eddie seemed to get depressed, "Well, no disrespect Mister Jimmy, but if being you actually sucks, I don't think I want to work for you. I mean what's the point?"

I watched Eddie walk off attempting to shrug the new found weight of the world from his lean young shoulders, shaking his head as he made it down to the street. I found out from some of my new hires over the course of the next year that Eddie was a problem resident at the halfway house and had difficulty dealing with the lady that ran the operation. I would catch him panhandling on occasion, but he always managed to make me smile.

I liked Eddie. I knew that the ex-cons he roomed with occasionally beat him up for stealing their food and that he had to be watched. But, after our first encounter he was no longer rude to my female staff. He was also not prone to intimidate customers when he did beg money from them. There was something sweet about him. However, he was a feral child, and like a domesticated kitten cast into the world, once he got some time in on the street some of the 'cute' began to wear off.

## The Last Panhandler on Earth

The double-blizzard of 2010 drove your ordinary panhandlers into shelters; back to mom's basement, and to the verge of extinction. But Eddie was made of tougher stuff. With two feet of snow on the ground I kept the store open into the second blizzard with a few employees. We largely serviced public works and emergency people. So when Eddie showed up to hustle on the store front I told him to keep it outside and let him have at the customers. These were all men, so I wasn't letting him have at old ladies or girls. Even so, this was a lapse. I should have been deposed by a more draconian Khan. Thanks to the state of emergency my shameful mercy was not noticed, and my heartless reputation was not besmirched.

As I was leaving the store that stormy Wednesday evening Little Eddie Horn was there on the sidewalk, wanting to get in the front door to spend the money he had begged from our last customer. We were the only two souls in sight, quite a change from our normal venue. Eddie had a ball cap crusted with ice, a snow-crusted windbreaker, torn jeans, and canvas tennis shoes with wet socks. This was a nastier storm then the last one, with more wind and sleet mixed with the snow.

I said, "Get lost Eddie."

He pleaded, "Please Mister Jimmy, I'm hungry?"

"Then starve Eddie!"

"But Mister Jimmy, that's not fair! You're not gonna starve are you Mister Jimmy?"

I then pushed my face into his and snarled, "Eddie I'm gonna spend the night with a fat woman—does that sound like starving to you!"

"No Mister Jimmy" he said as snot ran down over his chin and froze into an ice sickle, "that sounds kind of nice. Can I come with you?"

I snarled more deeply into his face, "Eddie when I hit that street down there at the edge of the parking lot, I'm not Mister Jimmy anymore, just the guy that will jump up and down on your scrawny ass—don't follow me!"

I limped off into the snowstorm with Little Eddie Horn standing under the canopy on the sidewalk; wondering what to do, where to go. He did not follow me. For you bleeding hearts out there [Mom, Siss, Aunt Madeline] I would like to report that, despite my best Cain-like efforts at social antipathy, Eddie survived somehow. A week later, at Belvedere and Loch Raven, he was following this big light-skinned dude around the bus stop, quizzing him about what it was like growing up as a light-skinned black man. At one point, as the gentle giant continued his unsuccessful efforts to evade Eddie, the little man-child panhandler who had survived the apocalypse declared, "I feel your pain brother. I used to be a black man too. And they kicked me out because I look Latino."

The bemused man looked at me, "Is he joking? How is this dude still alive?"

I just laughed.

## My Country Too

On a cool Sunday night in May I was informed that a panhandler had a customer blocked inside of his car. When I emerged from the store in my white shirt, black khakis, and ill-fitted tie, I saw Eddie begging a tall man who was still seated in his driver's seat, unable to stand up as he was being crowded so closely. The guy looked at me and I nodded to him as I approached Eddie. It looked like the fellow just wanted to get off the lot so I set my sights on getting Eddie way from the car.

I said, "Hey Eddie, step away from the man."

He did not respond and kept chatting up the customer.

I got closer, "Eddie, leave the parking lot, now."

Eddie then turned on me with a malicious fire in his dark eyes, "It is my country too Mister Jimmy. You don't get it all!"

Eddie was not directly over the man any longer. However, the fellow was still unable to close his car door. Eddie was pacing and agitated. After over 2,000 documented confrontations with people like

Eddie on this property I made a mistake. I should have taken my time but acted impatiently.

I grabbed a hold of the left sleeve of Eddie's gray hooded sweatshirt at the shoulder with my right hand.

He snarled and snatched my right wrist with his right hand.

The man slammed his door shut and sped off as I grabbed Eddie's right wrist with my left hand.

Eddie snarled again and closed with me, grabbing my left wrist with his left hand.

A middle-aged white woman was now passing us as Eddie snarled again and began to push me back toward the store front.

I was really surprised that this 120 pound kid was stronger than I. I wanted to let go and light him up with a combination but I was working, not at the bus stop. As he cranked up his retard strength and drove me toward the loading zone I crossed his arms over his chest and head-butted him between the eyes.

He let out a yelp as the woman exclaimed, "Oh God!" and hurried back to her car.

Eddie pulled away, "Why did you have to go and do that Mister Jimmy?"

"Eddie, you have to leave. You cannot hassle our customers!"

I then opened up my cell phone and dialed 911, "I'm calling the cops Eddie. You need to leave."

Eddie seemed hurt emotionally as he rubbed his forehead, "You know how to use it now, don't you Mister Jimmy."

"Leave Eddie."

By this time I was talking to the dispatcher and Eddie was walking off the lot promising to come back. He was not threatening, just adamant that he had a right to work the lot.

I stood on the storefront and waited for the responding officers as the police helicopter flew in from the Eastside. A regular customer of mine, an administrator at John's Hopkins University, stood with me and watched the process. Eventually there were three police cars and the chopper at the entrance to the lot when Eddie returned defiantly from up the road, wanting nothing more than to express his freedom by way of drinking some other retailer's beverage on Mister Jimmy's parking lot.

The lady cop asked me what I wanted done with him. Is said, "Miss we just wrestled and he got the worse of it. I just don't want him on the lot."

She smiled, "He has emotional issues. We'll just send him on his way."

When Eddie walked on he did not seem angry, but hurt.

I still feel bad for head-butting him.

The following Tuesday morning I was in Eddie's neighborhood, around the corner from the group home he lived in, waiting for the bus in front of the competing food store, where I had chased the half dozen panhandlers that now formed a picket-line at their parcel pickup railing. I never put on the hated management tie until I got to work, which strangely rendered me anonymous to most people on the bus stop. I had just begun writing my first novel and was proofreading a chapter as I sat on the bench waiting for the out-of-town bus. Then I heard a soft slight voice, "Excuse me sir, do you have the time?"

I looked over to see Eddie, who, as usual, when I ran into him on buses and bus stops, seemed to have no idea who I was. Before I became a store manager I would never even give people the time when I was out and about. For some reason, this had gradually changed, and I was actually glad to be able to help out Eddie in this small way, as he wondered if he had missed his bus, "It's eleven-o-four; nine more minutes until the bus comes."

Eddie nodded as he looked straight ahead into the hillside across the street, "Thank you sir."

Since that time I have occasionally thought that I saw Eddie boarding a bus from a distance at Belvedere and Loch Raven. But with Eddie, I could never be sure it was him until he opened his mouth. He just looked so much darker than he sounded that I could never really be sure it was him until he started running his mouth in that engagingly antisocial manner that always left me smiling. I hope Eddie Horn is off the streets, and, more importantly, that he has escaped the Big-butt Tyranny he so railed against the day we met.

## KayJay, Crumb & Millatime, Movin' on Up

© 2013 James LaFond

Panhandling begins in our society with the venerable lunch money shakedown of old, an extortion racket that is probably as old as American public education itself. Before we get into panhandler attempts at upward mobility [I've been paying attention Peter Joseph. Note the egalitarian spin already applied to this ghetto foray.] let us profile a former victim of the lunch money extortion racket, who has climbed the ladder of corporate success, despite having begun life as a skinny little Jewish kid running from gangs of black kids in West Baltimore...

**Addicted to Speed**

KayJay is a handsome thirty-something man with Leave it to Beaver black hair, who recklessly drives a ridiculously fast sports car, with a collection of speeding ticket stubs in the glove box. I noticed early on in our work relationship that KayJay was very athletic in a stiff way, with a perfect BMI. His stiffness was related to a stutter that was brought on by some sort of anxiety attack.

We were all thrilled one day to find out that our new assistant manager was the fastest retail food manager on Planet Earth! Big Bob and KayJay were wrestling some slimy crack-head in the vestibule who was trying to make off with crab meat. When that thief wormed his way loose and popped up and ran. Bob was like, 'No way are we catching that crack-head'. But KayJay took off and ran down that bag of chemically baked humanity like a falcon taking a pigeon on the wing. KayJay's running form was somewhat unconventional and spastic, and could be described as half-way between Forest Gump on steroids and Woody Allen on crack.

Sometime later KayJay drove me home at blinding speed in his coveted sports car. It occurred to me then that this man was addicted to speed. While I got my bearings in front of the LaFond Mancave—being afraid of cars to begin with—I asked him about it and he rattled off his racing resume, "I was the only Jewish kid in a black neighborhood. So I was supposed to give up my lunch money on the way to catch the school bus. Fighting a mob was useless, besides I was a little guy. So I ran. I'm faster than nine out of ten bush bunnies so it became a thing, a big event for everyone, like this sacred catch and release ritual; 'catch that Jew! Damn dat Jew boy can run!'

"Every once and a while I would get caught; like when they brought in a specialist. You had to be special to catch me.

"Even the bus driver got in on it. He wouldn't stop for my stop, because he didn't want all of those kids piling on behind me. He would slow down a little and just keep cruising with the door open, a crowd of black kids chasing me, and all of the other kids on the bus—you know they were all black—yelling, 'Catch dat white-boy, catch dat-white-boy'; and I'd leap on without breaking stride. And some crack-head thinks he's going to outrun me, the fastest Jew in Baltimore! Bring it!"

I really liked KayJay. Please say a prayer for KayJay, because 'The Fastest Jew in Baltimore' has been transferred to the Washington D.C. ghetto, a place feared by even West Baltimore's hardiest hood rats.

*[For one of KayJay's crack-head chases read Running from the Cops #1.]*

Now let's look in on another variety of interracial rundown...

## Crumb

The name Crumb is a diminution of the African-American slang term 'Cracker', itself a dismissive term for labeling 'inconsequential white folks'. Crumb was low on the Harm City Social Register indeed!

Crumb was a small slinky looking longhaired white-trashian, a stay-behind dope-fiend in the recently ebonicized Northeast Baltimore ghetto. He was just a grungy panhandler that I ejected from the storefront with some regularity. Now, retail food establishments who cater to a black clientele have their busiest rush right after church lets out early Sunday afternoon.

One fine spring Sunday I was just arriving to work when I noticed my assistant, a former cop, waving goodbye to a police cruiser. He told me that Crumb had tried upgrading to purse-snatcher. He grabbed the purse of an elderly lady who was wearing her Sunday dress and meema hat right behind register #4. Not only did Crumb kick off this audition for the Darwin Award in front of my armed assistant, but in the midst of over 50 church-going folks and their sons. In fact, her son, a large suited man in his thirties who used to play football, took great offense to Crumb scooting off at a negligible pace in his filthy attire with his mother's purse, and heroically gave chase.

The chase progressed down the sidewalk of the busy thoroughfare, with Crumb loosing pace and Mee-ma's son getting winded, but keeping up the chase. Crumb had given his pursuer an edge though. You see, the neighborhood east of the store was predominantly populated by white stoners like him and elderly folks who couldn't catch a cold let alone a junky. The neighborhood to the west of the store was predominantly black and was, and still is, roamed by gangs of black boys—some of them purse-snatchers themselves.

Yes, Crumb ran west!

As Meema's son chugged along, loosening his tie as he tried to keep pace with Crumb, he signaled a group of boys ahead. And, well, my assistant described the ensuing retrieval of Meema's purse as reminding him of the movie 'Zulu Dawn'.

The cops eventually extracted the remnants of Crumb from the 'feeding frenzy' and whisked him away to Central Booking, where he could be properly worked over by some heavy-handed brothers in lockup. My assistant had no doubt that other detainees would find out about the nature of Crumb's heinous offense.

I love a good vigilante story, and I am not done.

**Millatime**

*[The back-story in the first three paragraphs was had from an informed though 'shady' source and may or may not be true. The event that follows is pieced together from a radio news report, an officer's statement to the author, and a neighbor's third-hand account had from the Mother of the House. The incident occurred in the late 1990s, and has been cited in one of my earlier books.]*

Millatime was a small scrawny white stoner who scrounged in black Southwest Baltimore but lived in white South Baltimore. These guys tend to be tolerated by the locals because they infuse the economy with drug buys. They just have to make certain that they limit their activity in the host neighborhood to ground scrounging, panhandling and pimping out their girlfriend. If they start stealing they are rewarded with a free ride to the ER.

Millatime earned his unfortunate sobriquet when he was ground scrounging for unfinished beer up by Wilkens and Monroe *[Above where Sleepy was stabbed by the white boys from Pig Town in The Logic of Steel]*. Now, this activity would have predictably earned him a despicable moniker like 'backwash' if he had not done the Harm City Street-naming Committee one better. He—whatever his name used to be—found a bottle of Miller High Life beer, 'a 24-ouncer bottle with the twist-back-on-cap' that was nearly full with the fine yellowish pilsner. It was kind of warm since it had been sitting out on the median, and was a little flat. But it was beer—or perhaps it just used to be beer...

In any case, the low down was, that this prank by a Southwestern alcoholic drove Millatime to raise his game. In a desperate attempt to claw his way up out of the gutter, he used a relative's house as his criminal launch pad.

Houses in some parts of South Baltimore are divided every half a block by a deep dark alley a mere two to three feet wide. A friend of mine used to sneak from his mother's bedroom window into the bedroom window of the married woman who lived next door while the 'old man was still finishing his coffee in the kitchen downstairs'. Of course, my friend had the help of the housewife who opened her window for him when her husband went downstairs to head out to work.

Millatime had to break into 'the Three Bears' House', and they were always home. He decided, with a stroke of genius that would be quite beyond the ability of Crumb up in the Northeast, that he would not only use the cover of darkness, but break in on the third level—that is two levels up from the main floor—while the family of large pro wrestling fans were watching and cheering to a program known as 'Raw', aired on a weekday evening around 10 PM.

As Millatime worked the third story window of the Three Bears' House, they drank beer and snacked below, while Mom sat in her chair. [There is no indication that she was a fan, and this may have been his undoing.] Unfortunately for our upwardly mobile panhandler hero, he landed not so catlike on the ancient poorly maintained floorboards above as a loll in the action and Mom's keen house-honed ears conspired to alert the three very large pro wrestling fans; Dad, and two well-fed adult sons.

Mom called 911 to report an intruder while Dad and sons stormed upstairs to repel the enemy. It was ten or fifteen minutes before the police got there to rescue Millatime from the attentions of the wrestling fans. When asked what the men were doing to poor Millatime the officer I interviewed— who was not one of the responding officers—said, "I heard they were doing pile-drivers and something called 'The Peoples' Elbow'. What-the-hell is 'The Peoples' Elbow?'"

You know, sometimes the world I see around me gets me down a little. But today, after a trip down memory lane with KayJay, Crumb and Millatime, Harm City is looking okay to me.

## Gotham: Another Case for the Panhandler Genocide

© 2013 James LaFond

A few times a year a New York friend stops in town and hands me a pile of New York Post, and rare finds from the used book store scene. The story I am about to relate is adapted from the New York Post, Tuesday, December 4, 2012, page 4. It is an old tale as well, six months gone now. But when you go through life in the Luddite Lane this is how you get out-of-town news. You might consider this piece an addendum to The Case for the Panhandler Genocide, for which, I have yet to be nominated for the Nobel Peace Prize—you bleeding heart Europeans!

## Pan...Handling the Indignant

Fifty-eight year old Queens resident Ki Suk Han, had argued with his wife, had a few drinks, and left for the subway station. As he arrived he noticed that a crazed, filthy panhandler, about twenty years his junior, and taller and broader as well, was harassing commuters for change as they waited for the Q train headed downtown.

The older man approached the panhandler [one witness said aggressively, and others said in the interest of protecting others] and tried to calm him down. He was heard saying, 'You're scaring people'.

The panhandler said, 'You don't know me! You don't know who I am!'

A freelance Post photographer later described seeing a body fly through the air. It was Ki Suk Han, tossed down onto the rails as the Q train approached. The driver was not able to stop in time and Han, scrambling out of the concrete chute, was dragged fifteen feet and 'crushed...like a rag doll'.

Meanwhile the panhandler was heard saying 'Goddamn motherfucker' as he picked up his change cup and fled.

In a just world Han would have been Chung Lee and the panhandler would have been squished by the train. Of course, we live in an unjust world, and you need to look out for yourself, even when looking out for others. I have no way of knowing the exact circumstances. I can tell you this, about a third of panhandlers may escalate to violence in response to a show of weakness by a target, or, *in response to verbal aggressive by a third party.*

## Panhandler Nation

About a third of the hundreds of panhandlers that I have interdicted as a store manager have gotten aggressive with me. Of the thousands of panhandlers that have solicited me over the last three decades I can recall being hyper-aggressive towards them for a three year period when I was shedding what was left of the civilized veneer my mother had managed to lacquer on in my childhood. At 150 panhandlers a year for three years we come to a total of 450 that I stepped over, threatened, went after, chased, and snarled at. I actually robbed one mooching maggot and then threw his money in the sewer. I felt really bad about it until another scumbag began screaming at me for money while I was on my way to work in the freezing cold, to work in a freezer, for a cold ruthless bastard who stole money out of my check by editing the payroll program...

...Yes, thank you, I feel better now.

In any case, of the guesstimated 450 lowlifes that I was barbarically rude to; who I stepped over as they clung to life on the frozen sidewalks of South Baltimore, only two of those dudes threatened me back. This has a lot to do with self-justification of aggression. The begging maggot knows he is wrong; sells his soul on a minute-by-minute basis, as he grovels for your misplaced charity. When you lash back, if you have the requisite physicality—and more importantly that rusty hammer you carry to work to bang the wheel pins back into the forklift legs—to lend weight to your indignation, they back-off. They have no self-respect to begin with. Unless they are swarming in zombie mode or juiced up, 'back-off pal' is an easy sell.

## Their Soft Deserving Prey

Conversely, when this degenerate shred of humanity rises from the effusive gutters that spawned him to harass some easy target, someone who deserves to be preyed upon, and you interfere with that—well now, that is different. You see when he approaches someone who can smash his face in he is like the dog that just barks to see if you are afraid, and will never attack unless you run. But once he has homed in on some soft juicy guilt bucket in a suit or dress, he is on the hunt, maybe even primed to escalate from begging to demanding, to threatening, to force. He is no longer a barking dog, but a famished wolf, and your, are messing with his meal! If you can't convince him that you can and will beat him down you have a fight on your hands.

To begin with, even though he does not deserve to breathe our air, he is tougher than we are.

So you think he is not tough, because he proved unable to handle the daily stress that squeezes the humanity out of you like paste from a tube?

Do you sleep on concrete?

Do you have to knock hard crust off of your biological drainage device just to relieve yourself?

# Panhandler Nation

Do you fish pizza crust chewed on by hookers out of the gutter, wipe off the grease and lipstick with your filthy paws, and then eat it?

It doesn't take a genius to see where this all heads. You have just backed a really big smelly rat into a corner. Believe it or not, when it comes to our own real world zombies, the congealed human puss of the Urban End Times, you are better off with your back to a wall, and their back to the street.

Pushing someone into traffic is a classic defensive maneuver. A friend of mine killed a violent criminal by shoving him in front of a bus. I once punted a pit bull that was menacing me into a busy city street—and believe it or not the yuppies speeding through the ghetto on the way to their ivory tower office jobs swerved out of the way and risked their own lives to save that neck-ripping machine that had just run up on me. In a just world that unemployed four-legged prize-fighter would have landed in a yuppie lap and drained the Starbucks from his throat. As it was my welterweight quads did not pack enough punt to gain much lift, so my white-dappled brown foe whirly-skidded across two asphalt lanes and smacked into the curb, fixing me with an indignant look, before rejoining his pack and slinking away.

This brings us back to the beginning. Do not defend people against panhandlers unless the targeted person is with you, and is also your dependent [Mom, the wife, your daughter]. That way the justification is on your side. Even whack job panhandlers generally need to feel they are in the right. The guilt-rags who hand over change and the cowards who cringe or scurry away, have already justified his pursuit. They deserve to be intimidated; have indeed begged for it themselves.

Panhandling is his job. Do not mess with a man's job. He is working harder for his money than the people who own us, and he knows it. He has dropped out of Your World, and, if you defend yourself he will retreat back to the lonely trash-blown margins he inhabits like the undead creature he is. But if you try to bring Your World to him; invade his last vestige of dignity, unsavory as it may be, look out.

I might want to live in a world where we have 'panhandler season' in Baltimore just like we had 'buck season' in Western PA. But even if my fantasy comes true, and the dregs of the ghetto who have occasionally chased me through the cold nighted streets pining for the coat off my back, and have attempted to make me feel guilty for working hard at every turn, are reduced to the status of hunted animals, I would not underestimate such feral prey, and neither should you.

By the way, if this article has upset you, do not purchase **When You're Food**. I wrote the whole book in a period when I was repeatedly threatened while on my way to work, and while I read over a stack of decade old interviews with crime victims. That process brought out the darkness within that has sustained me well in the face of my subhuman enemies on the streets of Baltimore. An hour ago, when I sat down to read that six-month-old out-of-state paper before I lay down to sleep, I glanced at the cover and all that darkness came back. Looking now at the hauntingly dark photo of Ki Suk Han gazing into the headlights of the metal monster that is about to crush the life out of him, I am reminded that we are all a mere moment away from being food.

Oh, can you spare some change Big Guy?

'Excuse Me Sir, My Fetus is Jonesing'

© 2013 James LaFond

Today Cory and I were pulling out of Jim
Frederick's Kenpo into traffic, discussing a
gladiatorial Christmas theme ride that would have
him sitting in the economy car that he outweighs,
with a trunk full of dollar store goodies for the
hood-rat yutes, cracking the whip on me as I towed
the thing in a yoke under an antler-crested
helmet...when something even more absurd
stepped into view.

Right in front of the now closed diner made famous
by filmmaker Barry Levinson, a hundred yards
down the street from the more fit panhandlers that
have squeezed out the pawn shop sign spinners,

was a pregnant waif, walking the dotted line with a cardboard sign, raking in the dough from the guilt ridden suburbanites even as they fled the onslaught of food stamp week in the cars they shall never own.

This unsavory babe was literally stopping traffic with her half-covered incubator. Before the big man muscled his ailing vehicle into traffic 'Mom' was walking down the sidewalk counting and sorting her bills into denominations with her cardboard sign under her arm.

Every week for the past two months a shop in this suburban strip closed. Since March across Northeast and East Baltimore fulltime white trash panhandlers—the grungy Ted Nugent-on-crack looking ones that push old school black wino bums and insane fat bag-women onto the bus stops— have been proliferating. The normal count of one panhandler on the Kane Street Ramp has increased to three, working in shifts and handing off signs, for a total of six to nine guilt vectors. All across town, as our Master's Macroeconomist Puppets announce our improving employment rates on Sunday Morning Corporate TV, the once blonde-haired e-coli of our postindustrial bowels are overflowing the ghetto toilet bowel to expand their groveling stain—and that reproducing skank on Joppa Road, two miles from the Baltimore County Seat and a horse farm, was using tight jeans and a mid-drift shirt in an attempt to make it sexy!

Why not, it's a growth industry. Next to corrections officers I think panhandlers are the fastest growing segment of our service economy. Please, can we resurrect Roger Gorman and have him institute the Death Race? Would that require a constitutional amendment? Jason Statham can still drive the coolest car...

Perhaps some enterprising brats might hire these bums to dress up in North Korean uniforms and release them on a paintball course with helmet cams?

Couldn't some of you rich golf-playing twerps hire these people to dress up as giant gofers and carry your clubs for that snotty kid that tells you how to hit the ball and with what club?

Please, expiring minds want to know what your solution to this two-legged hood-rat plague could be, and how it could enrich some interestingly flawed creep, who we might then elect in place of our current flock of drool political drones.

Eureka, that's it, she had the answer all along: pregnant white trash stripers with dirty feet!

Harm City is safe for yet another day.

6/8/13

## Chiquita Madre Bes' not be Hatin' on Miss Ezz

© 2013 James LaFond

I just received a call from an Estrogen Alliance ghetto grocer who took me to task for not being hard enough on panhandlers! Imagine that, LaFond the Losertarian...

The call was rushed and she was 'fired up' over my glorification of the pregnant panhandler in Panhandler Nation #5. So here are the bits and pieces of her neoconservative rant as best I could scribble them down.

"I was a liberal until my forties. But by the time I hit forty I was looking around and saying to myself, 'Check this out, there is something wrong with this.'

"I wasn't a Christian but I was a bleeding heart. I would have been one of those people pulling over on the interstate ramp and rolling down their window to give money to the crack-heads. The

Mexican chick on Thirty-third and Hillen really burns me up; there every day like it's her job! This loser has a cardboard sign with pictures of her five kids on it. Now that's a lot of sex—where is he at? 'Not now! This isn't the time sister.'

"I keep my window up and shake my head. I'll only roll it down to say 'Get a job!'

"'You're hitting me up at the wrong time sister. The government is already giving you this and that, and the other thing out of my pocket, and you are going to double-dip on me! Not only double-dip on me but lie to me! Besides, you're hitting me up on my way home from Purgatory, buried in ghetto bullshit; and I just want to get home—away from this hellhole!'

"Now, the Beer Guy, with the beer sign. He's honest. I'll give money to him. Besides, all he has is AA; he's not on a methadone program. Even the crack-head, if he paints a sign 'need money for crack' I'll give to him. Sure, he's double-dipping but at least he's not lying to make me feel guilty for his bullshit.

"Back in the day I was the girl that would give out change. Now I'm the mean old lady that they right songs about for not caring. I'm scraping by and I'm supposed to help an addict buy drugs! Please. One day I might get my window cracked for saying, 'Get a job sister', but then it's on! Maybe I'll get the homeless shelter [phone] number and put it on my windshield next to my own 'Get a job!' Sign.

"I'm slaving away in the ghetto here, putting up with all of this shit, and I'm supposed to pay your way—it ain't happenin' sista. En ya know that's right!"

"I finished the conversation by noting an old truism, 'That people who are conservative before thirty-five are heartless, and those who are liberal after thirty-five are stupid.'

In response Miss Ezz said, "Now that makes me feel a little better. I wasn't a heartless bitch then and I'm not a bimbo now."

## Barefoot and Bearded in Paradise Found

© 2013 James LaFond

Yesterday morning, that is Sunday June 16, I was wending my way through the ghetto out to Paradise Found to have breakfast with a historian and educator who has kind of adopted me as a pet brain. I began with a one mile trek through the ghetto, thankfully silent as the hood-rats and white-trash slept the slumber of the stoned. At the bus stop I read a V. J. Waks novel about a killer mutant babe while a middle-class black youth eyed me with obvious fear; bald and dressed in black steel-toe boots and black cargo shorts with a sleeveless shirt, arms sporting razed stick welts from yesterday's sparring.

'Being trash has its perks', I mused as a squad of rats from Fire Base Doritos rummaged through the corn chip and cheese curl bags at my feet for their Sunday morning repast.

'No panhandlers—nice.'

I transferred buses at a suburban shopping center, and boarded behind an angry ghetto girl that was rude to the middle-aged male driver, who I made certain to be respectful to. This driver had a thing for the forced 'good morning' making sure to make you feel like a heel if you did not promptly say good morning. This is a bit unfair, as bus patrons are so conditioned to always put on a hard face to frustrate strong-arm robbers interviewing potential victims and to discourage the legions of panhandlers, who were thankfully absent here as well.

I returned to Ms. Waks' book only to be interrupted by a blazing example of virulent white trash. The man had boarded the bus, attired in sleeveless shirt and cargo shorts with backpack just like I, and then began shouting at the driver who had the gall to be courteous. He was acting angry, even psychotic, turning on the bus driver, "Leave me alone and do your job sir. You work for the MTA and the MTA works for me. I don't have to kiss your ass any more than I have to kiss her ass right there!" he wolfed, pointing at the angry ghetto girl who was angry no more, and shifted restlessly in her seat.

I was getting angry at this guy because I knew, and everybody on this bus knew, that he was only getting racially ballistic on this bus because he and I had parity with the two black males on this bus. Deep in the hood, at 15 to 1 odds he would have mumbled 'Good morning sir' and slinked to his seat. But here he was a badass. I suppressed the urge to slam his head against the window, and went back to my book.

Fifteen minutes later I offloaded, and made certain to wish the driver a 'Happy Fathers' Day.' But he had soaked up enough white hate this morning to make his reply stiff and forced. Unable to make things right I returned to my Darwinian mindset, and then recalled, 'I am in Paradise Found, not a combatant within five miles. I can wander about in this postindustrial service economy wonderland without concern.'

I read as I walked across the lot to the food market. As I made the entrance a skinny middle-age black woman was cussing out a grungy white barefoot panhandler, "Fuck you boy, fuck yo-all nigger!"

I selected some almond milk and took my time picking out the cereal. As I checked out, and checked out the twenty-something woman buying baby food—I know, that is wrong on multiple levels—I noticed that my cashier was a handicapped African woman who could barely reach the scanner. As my Darwinian ethics continued to desert me, even to the point where I discontinued my ogling of the fertile young lady, I broke down and donated a dollar to some bleeding heart cause or another—even attempting to sign my name on the donation slip with my oft-broken hand.

'What', I asked myself, 'would the Great Khan think of me now?'

'Am I a woman—albeit a dyke—destined to descend into a living hell of effusive misplaced compassion?'

'Have I lost my edge?'

'Will I actually give money to that bum outside when I pass him by?'

'Please', I prayed to the cruel and heartless Nordic ancestor that I sincerely hoped lurked somewhere in my genome, 'let me have the strength to despise the weak, to cast a dark shadow across their—No, I'm getting soft; can't even muster a soul-damning curse!'

I smiled pathetically at the struggling woman behind the counter; as much impaired by her physiology as I was by the bleeding-heart ethics somehow brought to the surface by Mister Good Morning the bus driver.

Out the door I went.

I was headed for the panhandler, whose grungy little hand even now was receiving a dollar bill from a well-dressed black business man who walked like an athlete. I raised the book to read as I walked and headed toward the begging zone, hoping that I would not be tried, that the author of The Case for the Panhandler Genocide would not show the yellow streak!

The dirty feet under the too long jeans retreated behind the propane locker and I walked on reading about mutant babe Gerda Tau eating some scientist alive. Then, as I hit the begging zone I heard its plaintive voice, "Excuse me Sir, I don't mean any disrespect, but could you spare some change?"

He sounded pathetic, broken—nice even. I stopped and closed my book, looking over at him with the same narrow gaze I had given the youth at the ghetto bus stop hours before, and he had the same reaction, swallowing hard, and stepping back. Only he was more pathetic, burying his hands in his pockets and rounding his shoulders, looking teary-eyed at me from under his brows. He had a wife-beater shirt on, representing a venerable American institution that he was surely incapable of continuing. He had long soft brown hair in a ponytail, a lazy or damaged eye, and a wimpy half-assed go-tee that could not conceal his weak chin.

I switched the book to my right hand and slid it into the side pocket of my cargo shorts to extract my wallet—I know, my portrait is being taken down from the Aryan Nation Compound fence even as you read this—and said, "Sure pal, I've got something for you."

As I extracted my wallet hope lit across his face—a fat wallet it was, stuffed with thirty ones and some more lofty bills as well. He actually stepped forward in a shaky manner, his shoulders shuttering a little, and pursed his mouth for the obligatory thank you.

Note: There is no way this guy survives a day on a major corner. The crack-heads would beat his ass and toss him over the guardrail into the drainage ditch below. He has found a niche though, where the worst he has to fear is some chick who hates her fast food job chewing him out.

I opened my wallet and slid out a brand new card, not plastic, but a business card. He seemed happy to see it. Perhaps I was a homeless advocate about to proffer a halfway house or shelter pass? Maybe I was a born again commiseration vector willing to feed him so long as he listened to my sermons, as my father had done with the bums he had scraped off of Baltimore City streets in the early 1970's?

He seemed confused when I handed him the Harm City card, so I said, "Look, when you save up enough change to buy a computer, go online, go to the Harm City page on that website, and scroll down to Panhandler Nation. By then you'll be famous."

I replaced my wallet in its proper place, and winked at him as he stammered, "Th-th-thank...you, sir..." and I walked away, hoping that I had effected a compromise that would please—or at least not invoke the wrath of—Genghis Khan and MomMom LaFond.

For readers concerned with 'Beard Boy' as I have affectionately named this most polite panhandler, I will make this promise: If I pass his way again I will pay him for an interview. If you are concerned with his plight please note how much money you think I should donate to his indigence, and any questions you would like me to ask on your behalf.

## The Day After Food Stamps

© 2013 James LaFond

It was midnight, January 18, the last day of food stamps in the ghetto. Thinking it would now be safe to go shopping late at night—with food stamp traffic tapering off sharply on the last day of largesse, and the alcoholics and drug addicts not yet panhandling in force—I had made my way to Shop & Beg. I did so on the advice of Cheap Guys R' Us Customer Service Manager Miss Ezz, who assured me, "That Mexican chick and her cardboard baby-picture sign will be off the corner for a week now. She'll be back though, as soon as she blows through those stamps. The losers should all be stuffing their guts with steamed shrimp and pop tarts—so if ever there was a time to go shopping it is right after the eighteenth."

As Fate would have it—and I think Fate now resides in a cardboard box behind an inner city bakery—many early food stamp recipients, who received their monthly dole between the 6th and the 10th were on hand, and I found myself stacked up behind them at the lone midnight register as they dug for change in their pockets and recounted the wadded up bills in their hands.

First was the female dope fiend, covered in tattoos and wearing a wife-beater and dirty sweatpants that had no seat over the left cheek, which was not sealed with antimicrobial panties as it should have been. She was perhaps 35, though it is hard to tell with addicts. I think she was a crack-head. She was shopping with three men in their twenties who had to pool their money to purchase their Honey Nut Cheerios and 48 ounce jug of fake orange juice.

This left no money for mamma's cigarettes, so she got on the federal cell phone and began hitting up a fourth male for 'change', with the following woeful plea, "I be broked yo. Ya needz ta front me some change."

The young men left, but she hung around on the sidewalk awaiting a car...

In the mean time 'Our House' the two middle-aged white trashians who are recovering meth-heads but still spend most of their time drunk, including this night, were bickering in line about the grocery bill, which consisted primarily of canned cat food. As another man hovered near by curiously the half of the duo who still had human looking skin started threatening us with the possible ramifications of his not being able to pay the bill, "Somebody needs to help with this cat food bill. I have eleven cats en if I can't feed them I'm goin' to set them loose on the neighborhood!"

The newcomer rifled through his pockets and spoke up, "Here yah go—we used ta do meth under the bridge."

Meanwhile the crack-ho had been picked up by a car out front.

By the time these stumblebums had completed their transaction and related stoner gossip, which consisted of talking about the late 1980s as if it were last week, I was finally on cue to have my chocolate milk rung up. The cashier winked at me and nodded to the departing stoners, "Friends of yours?"

"No man."

He then scanned the milk and considered the happy looking cow on the bottle, "Is this your favorite; you get this a lot."

"Oh it tastes pretty good. The reason I prefer this brand though is the comforting notice on the side of the bottle that assures me that there is no measurable nutritional difference between organic milk and milk from cows treated with hormones— I'm in training, 'roiding' up you might say."

"Oookaaayyy," he said as he bagged my milk and made change.

Just then, as he was wishing me good night, the crack-ho returned with a handful of mashed up ones, looking more haggard still, "I gotz yo baby; we flush now. I'll take da Newport Filta Kings...'

...and out the door I went.

I am giving Harm City tours for visiting dignitaries if you are interested.

## Investment Begging 101

© 2013 James LaFond

So you think hedge fund managers are resourceful scum?

If you like them, you will love Willy.

Last night I was sitting outside a Harm City pizzeria with Doc, who happens to be my doctor, and a good friend as well. I trust him not to crush my left testicle when I cough, and he trusts me not to write about his hellish life; to leave that to his own cathartic keyboard. We had been eating inside. When he noticed lowlifes skulking around his pickup truck—which had a full gas can in the bed— we moved out to the lush concrete-paved ground-level veranda that bordered on the asphalt lawn. We had eaten all but two slices of a large pizza with everything, and had just decided that he would take the survivors home rather than I taking them to work.

Just then Willy, a big dark-haired man who looks like Sam Elliott might have looked if he did as much dope as Keith Richards, turned the corner. He spied us at the table, scrounged for some change in his pockets, and then entered the Hindu pizzeria. Willy was not dirty, did not appear homeless. I'm fairly certain he lives in his 80 year old mother's basement.

Willy emerged from the shop with a 50 cent [Did you know there is no longer a cents symbol on the keyboard?] bag of chips. He then came over to us and asked if he could trade us the chips for a slice of pizza. Doc said, "Take it man—we're done."

Willy said, "Take the chips, man, really, I don't eat 'um."

Doc said, "It's our pleasure—we're done anyhow. Enjoy"

Willy took the chips and the pizza box, and his tenacious dignity, to the corner of the veranda and began to feast. He kept saying, 'Thank you man!' and Doc kept saying, 'Your welcome dude.'

Then a clutch of hood-rats ambled by, pushing a baby carriage with a food stamp vector in it, smoking cigarettes, which gave off mini smoke columns in the night as if the carriage were a diesel rig in miniature, belching carbon into the sky. Willy began screaming at them, "Give me a fuckin' cigarette! A fucking cigarette!!"

They continued on their way and he eventually approached us nervously; a peasant approaching two lords at their high counsel, "Would you gentlemen happen to smoke?"

We responded that we did not, that our athletic activities precluded any such reasonable use of our lung capacity. This got him thinking and he began wondering how long he had been a smoker, "Let me see, I started smoking the night I started snorting coke."

At this hint Doc began peering up into his nostrils apparently trying to rate the erosion and arrive at an estimated date of addiction...

As Willy ransacked the crevices of his brain for its history of demise a young lady rounded the corner and asked us for a light. Doc and I declared ourselves unlit as we both admired her curvy nineteen year old figure, neatly brushed hair, and Daisy Duke attire. It was about ninety degrees on the veranda. Willy checked her out with audible grunts and said, "I'll give ya a light if ya give me a cigarette."

Our Scarlet O'Hara held up an inch-and-a-half long gutter-scrounged cigarette butt and said, "This is all I've got."

Willy pounced, "Let's share!"

She jutted out her hip, "Okay man."

Willy took his time lighting the stump and managed to arrive at the same anonymous companionship calculus as we did. Namely, that if this chick was willing to swap spit with him and whoever had dropped that butt in the gutter for two puffs, then she would part with whatever was left of her dignity for a few bucks worth of booze.

Willy felt his pockets, his mental cue for the seeking of good will investment opportunities, and glanced first at my heavy work clothes and then at Doc's summer shirt, and dollar signs lit up in his eyes. Doc would surely be able to part with a twenty to assure Willy one final go at a still fully toothed companion. As he searched for the words and reached for the glowing ember of a butt Doc looked at me and said, "That's our cue."

We did not have the heart to stand around and savor Willy's desperate attempt at meaningless body fluid exchange. We just went our separate ways, no longer capable of being surprised by the rampant culture of addictive consumption that defines, this, the greatest nation to ever rule on earth.

You might look down on Willy and his gutter princess, but they are ready for the Zombie Apocalypse, and you are not!

Panhandler Nation

## Bad For Business

© 2013 James LaFond

Last night I found myself at a bar next to a woman who was hopefully drinking at the rate that would have me looking like Christian Bale within a few hours. As we bought another round a man who was actually shorter than I ambled up to the bar at my left shoulder and asked for a Samuel Adams. The imbibing babe by my right shoulder chuckled, "He's in the wrong joint! This is a Crudweiser hole-in-the-wall."

The man did settle for a Guinness stout and sat quietly taking in the sights and sounds of rampant inebriation among the city hicks to his left, as the older bachelors to the lady's right in the back of the bar talked about betting odds. Eventually the fellow commented on a boxing match on TV and was suddenly a person of interest.

112

His name is Sam, a mild mannered genteel man from Arlington Virginia who works in finance and somehow ended up in Harm City Central. He and his new wife are part of the urban re-gentrification process in this area. Sam began asking me for neighborhood information; seemingly out on a scouting expedition to determine the best and safest venues to bring his wife. It was not long before a Harm City business card was produced and Sam began relating some panhandler experiences...

## D.C. Guilt Merchants

Sam was at a traffic light in Washington D.C. when he noticed one of three panhandlers attempting to acquire the companionship of a lady who was light years out of his league. The other two panhandlers looked at each other holding their signs, and one said to the other, "We can't have this. He's bad for business!"

I for one am glad that D.C. has a panhandlers' union, and would like to invite them to open a locale in Harm City, which I will throw my inconsiderable political clout behind.

## The Underground Service Economy

Sam was driving into Baltimore one day and experienced the industry of a 'squeegie kid' who cleaned his windows for 'some change'. He then parked elsewhere and experienced the industry of a man who did something for him [The city hicks were howling a country western song and I missed that Sam.]. Sam then pulled into a gas station and was confronted by a man who just 'asked for some change.' "I felt my empty pockets, and then thought to myself, 'If there are going to be bills involved, or even just change, than this man should at least pump my gas.' By that point in the day I was already conditioned to patronize all of these informal activities. He needed to get with the program!"

So even mild-mannered Sam has something of the capitalist tyrant in him!

## Gas Can Man

"I was pulling onto an off ramp and this fellow is leaning out into the road, holding a gas can, declaring that he had broken down and needed some 'change' to help fill his gas can, so that he could fuel up his car. I just thought to myself, 'Now that is a very well-planned unforeseen occurrence. I do not haul a gas can around with me in case I break down.' It was at about that time that I realized that panhandling was a business, a job."

If I might speak on behalf of Baltimore panhandlers, When the D.C. Panhandler Union opens their locale in Baltimore I would like to nominate Sam as their accountant and investment analyst. I have your business card Sam! Expect a collect call from one of the seven surviving Harm City payphones anytime now.

## Unilaterally Cruel in High Heels

© 2013 James LaFond

*I've been saving this story since last Christmas for a holiday season post. This story features Miss Ezz, buxom head cashier at Cheap Guys R Us.*

"I was stopping for gas. It was about two in the afternoon. I had had a shit day at work. I can't remember why I had a shit day, just that it was a shit day. I'm walking from my car to pay with my purse over my arm and this skinny crack-head white-girl approaches me, 'Miss can you spare two dollars? My car is broken down around the corner and I need some gas.'

"I was in no mood. I stopped and look at her and said, 'I'm not giving you any money.'

"Then she gets indignant, 'I really need two dollars!'

"I was not in the mood, 'Well then sister you should have come up with a better bullshit story, then 'my car is broken down around the corner'. Do you think I'm stupid?'

"Now she was pissed and started coming closer calling me a bitch and telling me she needed money. I bent down, took off my high-heeled clog, and cocked it back, 'If you come one step closer girlfriend I will smack you upside your head and you will hit the floor sister! And you will not get up!'

"I was hot, ready to go. All I needed after a shit day was to have this crack-head white-girl druggie bitch giving me shit because she needed more drug money. I don't think so sister!"

"She ran her mouth some more, named me a few different kinds of bitch, and then took her nasty self off to do whatever else she does for her drug money—goodbye!"

*That is how a sister throws down in Harm City.*

Mo Coffee

**Homeless in Harm City**

© 2013 James LaFond

"I got a story ain't got no moral."

-Billy Preston

**The Heartless Blogger**

I was homeless for six weeks in 2003.

My new roommate Eric was homeless for about the same period earlier this year. [See Eric's Backpack below].

I have stepped over dozens of freezing homeless men, primarily in the late 1990s.

I have written 'The Case for The Panhandler Genocide.'

# Panhandler Nation

My column, 'Panhandler Nation' is largely a rant against the acquisitively homeless.

On the other hand I am a big fan of 17th Century pirates, Germanic nomad tribes, and Magyars, who were all essentially virulently covetous homeless folk.

So, what I am about to write may surprise you.

## Beyond the Ghetto?

As a food market clerk, working for Good Guys R' Us out in the county, I pulled three shifts in a row leading up to Thanksgiving. I normally do not work even two nights in a row. This afforded me the opportunity to see a rare and melancholy drama unfold.

This slice of the suburbs, ten miles beyond the Harm City line, is no longer pristine; has become a ghetto annex, a target of slothful imminent domain. The postmodern ghetto is an ever-expanding phenomenon, hollowing out at its core to make way for urban homesteaders of the nearly wealthy class, even as the parasitic hood-rats scatter in pursuit of the receding civilization that is their reluctant host.

Our store has been open for 24 hours since January. Doing this in the ghetto is suicidal on many levels, but is workable, here, far beyond the criminal epicenter of our society. The night captain discussed the eventual homeless encroachment of winter earlier this year, dreading the consequences and his inequitable role in the store policies that would surely ensue.

## Mo Coffee

On Monday night 11/25/13 I noticed a black man in late middle-age, wearing slightly dirty sweats and old sneakers, limping through the store to the coffee pot. He is suffering from the onset of a nervous system disorder of some kind. He is very dark and has a droopy swollen lower lip. His appearance alone was enough to evoke pity. I have worked predominantly on majority black night crews throughout my life.

I have noticed that dark-skinned men with large lips are often ridiculed by their peers. Even the big dangerous ones get picked on behind their back, so you know it had to be bad for this guy in childhood. I once worked with a multiple murderer with the street name of Mumblejack. This dude was super scary. Even so, the other black clerks would make fun of him constantly with sayings such as, "Dat nigga straight from Africa!" and "Sheee, dat nigga got lips bigga den Mick Jagga!"

I found much to pity about this man, particularly the fact that he was on the street during a blast of cruel winter weather. I also found some things to admire.

He kept his purchases spread out to about one an hour and then took his time consuming them on the bench up front. When he no longer had a legitimate purpose to be in the store he would pace out front on the sidewalk, staying out of the way of customers, and even cleaning up trash.

He never panhandled.

When Charlene bought him coffee, he thanked her, and did not come back to her again expecting a handout. He even wiped the counter around the coffee pot. When other customers were nearby, he made himself scarce, not wanting to be a nuisance.

I took to calling him 'Mo Coffee' as he hit the pot every hour for the 13 hours I was on the job. He noticed when we would come up front on our breaks to sit, and would go outside during these times. This dude was the perfect homeless guy. On Tuesday night, as I took my seat on the bench to finish reading V.J. Waks novel Hammerspace on my break, Bubba, our cashier, nodded to Mo Coffee, and said, "You took his seat. He's going to stay outside in the cold until you're done."

Bubba came over and leaned on the back of the idle register lane, "He's a nice guy. It's kind of nice having him around. But you can see Reggie [the night captain] keeping an eye on him. How long do you think he'll be okay here?"

"He hit the jackpot. He is a low-impact specialist, the rare self-sufficient homeless guy. He has money. He spreads it out to make sure he's welcome or at least tolerated. He doesn't beg. He's a strong dignified man. Most of us would be crying in the gutter in his shoes, knocking on mom's door, begging for a space on the couch. He has survival protocols and sticks to them."

Bubba seemed surprised that I was not calling for his homeless head, knowing that I had once been among the cruelest and least tolerant store managers in the area. He nodded again, "So you think management will let him stay?"

"I would have bounced him out on Monday. I was a heat-seeking missile where loiterers were concerned. He's Daniel Boone—the polite pathfinder. We are the Indians. Management is the chiefs. The panhandlers, muggers and thieves that have chased him out of the ghetto, they are the white soldiers coming to rape and pillage. You have to kill the pathfinder or drive him off, or you get overwhelmed. Zero tolerance is the only defense. You can't solve the problem. You can just move it down the street. When I took that management job there was always a panhandler on duty, about a half-dozen a day. When I resigned there were none, but the Aldis down the street had a picket line out front. When the store was open for business every gap in the bars was covered by a dude I had bounced off my lot."

Bubba seemed sad, "Happy days."

"That's what Reggie is dealing with. He's already upset about telling this dude to get lost next week, when it's even colder out."

Bubba seemed to be weighing the social scheme of things, and whispered, with a long look at Mo Coffee, "I like having him around. He's a nice guy."

On Wednesday night, I asked Bubba, "Where's our man?"

"John [the store manager] put him out."

Bubba was noticeably depressed by the encroaching darkness of the world. I said what I could to assuage the 19-year-old, "At least he saved Reggie from the guilt."

Bubba nodded and said wistfully as we looked out into the icy night, "I hope he found a place, at least to eat Thanksgiving dinner."

"Amen brother."

Longman

© 2013 James LaFond

On Monday morning, at 12:50, December 23, 2013, in front of Larry Flint's House of Smut, on Baltimore's 'Block', I arrived on Baltimore Street to connect to an out-of-town bus. Little did I know, in this misty morning twilight, that I was about to encounter an actual time-traveler. I, as a sci-fi writer, was both awed and honored. Permit me to regal you with a Harm City Christmas carol.

Few people were about at this hour. One gang banger walked by with his drunken ho on his arm. She looked at me, and looked up at the bus stop sign, then said, "What bus you waiting for baby?"

"The Twenty-three", I said.

She waived me off, grinned, and said, "Oh, it I'll be right here—you good baby."

Off she lean-walked with her Stringer Bell knockoff.

The usual bums were out of sight, as it was pretty wet out, between downpours. A few young people wandered about. There were no drunken Russian dudes trolling for black hookers. Then a very tall black man in his mid forties, wearing a knit cap, a windbreaker and jeans, approached me with a measured questioning look, "You okay brother— you good?"

This guy was not a drug-dealer. He was not being quiet, not waiting until he was close, as if he were a dope-slinger or a narc. I began to feel a bit of nostalgia for the early 1990s when panhandling was still an art, when creative down-and-outers tried to make a craft of being economically dead, literally clawing their way up from the gutter by making themselves useful to anyone who could spare some change.

Apparently this guy had not gotten the 1998 predatory panhandling memo, and was acting like he had just stepped out of a time capsule. Rather than me describe how upstanding panhandlers used to attempt to earn some of your change, let this man tell it.

He stopped before me, hands in his pockets, and looked up at the murky skyline, that I have always associated with wretched urban squalor, as if he were looking into a bright blue candy-cane sky.

"I love this night. I'm loving life brother. It is so good to be free, even if I don't have a place to pee."

I looked up at him, my Darwinian resolve already softened by his manner, and he continued, "I could take the train back to D.C. you know. You know they have that now. I just got out of prison—fifteen years brother, fifteen lonely, waiting years. This is paradise. Two bags of heroin—fifteen years! Dumbest day of my life."

"So you're from D.C."

"Yeah", he said, with a wistful look in his faraway eyes, "I used to cut the grass on the White House lawn. Can you believe that? Never again—that is dead and gone. Haven't found no work up in hear yet, but I'm looking. In the meantime, I'm looking out for people, in case they need anything."

"What was that like, working on the White House grounds?"

"Good, real good man, especially when Reagan was in there. The man would stop and waive, even say hello to you, and ask you how you were doing—like you were somebody even though you were just cutting the lawn. He was real nice like that. He bought people in my neighborhood some houses and moved them in. His wife was a bitch. But you know what? She looked out for her man. She protected his ass better than the secret service. If there had been an attack or some shit, she would a lined us up in front of him, would have thrown her own self in front of him. We missed him.

"Now Bush—the old one, not the dude who couldn't pronounce shit—he was okay, walk in and out, comin' en goin'."

"Clinton now, he was cool. Didn't see so much of him; you know, got that big girl under his desk and all!"

We laughed together and I couldn't let that go, "Did he ever come after you with that cigar?"

Longman laughed hard at that and put his arm around me, "You know I'm too tall to kneel under a desk now—wait, stand still."

Longman ducked down behind me like I was a hunting blind. A small Pakistani man of about college age was walking past to my left, trying to

light up a cigarette. Out Longman pounced, like a
character from a cartoon, leaping about ten feet and
slapping both hands down on the little man's
shoulders. The Pakistani fellow put his hands to his
heart and bugged his eyes out as he threw himself
back against the pawn shop window, screaming,
"Fuck! Fuck man—fuck you Longman!!"

Longman was now hugging him with one arm and
dragging him to me like he was a prize poodle, "You
see my foreign man here brother! I look out for him.
I got this my man."

He then took the man's shaking hand and produced
a lighter, lighting the man's cigarette. They then
hugged, and the small man addressed me, "I run
seven-eleven all night. Longman looks out for me—
help me good udder night."

Longman proudly flexed one arm as he hugged his
friend with the other, and said, "At forty-eight, I can
still roll. Joint keeps a dude fit", as he pointed to a
missing front tooth.

The convenience store clerk smiled and proudly
pointed to Longman with his thumb, "Twenty-four I
am, new country, late shift, good friend."

He then handed me his smart phone and asked me something I could not understand. Longman translated, "He wants you to take a picture of us—send it back to the sheik I suppose."

I managed, after three attempts, to snap a picture of the two men separated by two feet in height and a world of tradition. I wanted to ask them about the 'help' Longman had rendered but my bus was coming up. Longman put his hands on my shoulders, "Could you spare anything bro, any change? I'm saving up for breakfast."

"I'm sorry man. I got just enough to get me to work and back. If I see you again, I'll help you out."

He shook my hand, said he understood, and stepped out in the street to make sure the bus stopped for me. Before I stepped on board he patted me on the back and wished me a merry Christmas, even as his friend said, "I got you—let us go eat."

There was once a time when many panhandlers regarded it as their duty to try and do something for you, if only to entertain you with some conversation. Back then, even the useless ones would explain their addiction, itemize their woes, of at least had the decency to lie to you about their plight.

I'm thinking Longman has a niche waiting for him, until he can land a real job. He literally has no competition, as the panhandlers of today either whine, grouse angrily, threaten, pressure, or just stand zombie-like with a sign hanging from their neck.

I hope his friend is working at the Baltimore Street 7-11 tonight.

Have a warm Christmas.

## Harm City Hicks

### Painfully Sober Stoner Trash and A Trashed Motorist

© 2014 James LaFond

Last night I arrived at work on foot, after a serene bum-free walk out into the county, only to have some dirty blonde thirty-something redneck in a sweat-stained John Dere hat lean back slightly over the railing outside the egress point to my eight hours of low income toil, and grouse, "Spare any loose change? I'm tryin' ta get on this bus."

The last bus had just passed me. He obviously wanted to cop some crack from Yo Somoti behind the dumpster.

He had been fairly un-abrasive, so I answered as lazily as he had asked, "Nah."

As I entered he snarled over his shoulder, "Well fuck you too asshole!"

I smiled radiantly and headed to the time clock past a clan of morbidly obese twenty-something foodstampers and their milling spawn, as they heaped pop tarts, potato chips, tasty cakes and soft drinks on the register belt.

My boss has no balls and is not going to drive this scum off the lot. So there is no point in giving him a head's up. I just go to work. Panhandling Season is beginning to bud later than usual. It is still not enough to generate a new Panhandler Nation, which strikes a deep sorrow in my bleeding heart. If these bums don't start showing more initiative I'll have to dig into the Harm City archives for some old school panhandling tales.

Walking back toward the city, this morning at 6:52, a fine new vehicle, that seems a hybrid between an SUV, a station wagon, and a pickup truck, speeds by me doing about 40 MPH in a 25 MPH zone. Not looking up in time to see the motorist, I wonder if the local hicks are getting soft, or if the local upper crust white bread is getting wannabe gritty at the car lot. Then I hear a large booming pop. It sounds like a nine-millimeter report as heard from the breech side of the firearm in a concrete alley. Only this is five to six times the magnitude of an automatic handgun report.

I look for a truck backfiring before me and realize that the sound has echoed from the building ahead of me, but originated behind. I turned to see an overhead wire tangling in the gutter over a felled light pole and a small splintered tree. The vehicle is still moving, but appears to be just gliding down the incline toward the waiting curb where Eastern Avenue narrows by the park entrance. I have no idea what condition the front of the vehicle is in.

Once again forgetting that I was raised by two Good Samaritans, I do recall that I have a bus to catch, and that I would like to read a chapter in my Phillip Jose Farmer novel before it pulls up, and continue on down the sidewalk, content to be a pedestrian.

'Like Conquered Prey'

**Death Slap by Caitlin Nolan and Barry Paddock, New York Daily News, 5/24/14**

© 2014 James LaFond

Brooklyn Shane sent me a 'Check this out son!' heads up about this somewhat dated story which features sequential security camera stills from the front of a Bronx bodego.

A picture of a sober Italian/Swiss tourist is juxtaposed with a picture of an unkempt afro topped black man in a wife beater, stamped in red with WANTED. However, at the time of the incident the tourist was 'being obnoxious, bugging people for a drink.'

This fatal fight is of interest firstly because it was a fight, not an attack. Secondly, and most importantly, it is a demonstration of the effectiveness of the open hand.

As a news story this is top notch old time stuff the likes of which we never see in a literary news pit like Baltimore. I love New York street reporting. Caitlin and Barry scored a great interview with 'Frankie' a cagey eye-witness, and deserve credit for getting video stills.

The drunken tourist was walking around with a banana demanding that bodega patrons buy him booze. The afro guy stood up to him with hands behind back. The tourist then leaves, takes off his shirt, returns, and squares up to fight. The afro guy clocks him with what was said to be a slap. From the blurry film still it seems to be a left hook with a hard pivot behind it. It is hard to tell. The afro guy is definitely set for a killer cross as the tourist falls back to the pavement where his head will be dashed open and his ten day drunk wastefully ended.

I hope that the Death Slap dude shaved that hair and escapes detection. This is certainly reminiscent of the Korean karate master versus the black pimp from some hears back. Please note that there was a manhunt announced for the defender in this mutual combat. As much as this is an illustration of the effectiveness of slapping and cuffing, note that cut-off strikes and preemptive strikes make you—in the eyes of the law—the aggressor. If you let your ego get the best of you and stand to fight for such trivial matters, at least let the dude throw first, and then counter. It might help lessen the manslaughter charge.

Go to NYDailyNews.com and check out the video. What an excellent reporting job.

Big Roy and the Boy

**A Harm City Dialogue with Miss JoJo**

© 2014 James LaFond

I interviewed Miss JoJo at the courtesy window of the ghetto supermarket where she is employed, asking her casually about her food stamp cycle two full days after the EBT rush reached its crescendo on Wednesday the 16th.

"It was pretty much your usual, threw out my back lifting hundreds of forty-two pound boxes of chicken wings at the register. A lot of your normal EBT bullshit with the customer putting two-hundred dollars more on the belt than they have on their card. Most of the people are pretty nice. We did have this one ghetto bitch with her gangbanger boy friend who was a dollar twenty-nine short. She looks at her old man and says, 'I need two dolla.'

"He just looks at her, and she keeps asking rudely. Eventually she says 'please' and he pulls out this knot-roll of money as thick as your fist and peels off two ones; five-hundred and forty dollars of my tax money so that this drug dealer with ten grand in his pants can eat steak and shrimp. It's kind of sad that so few EBT people can add, not even up to five dollars. The women are the dumbest by a long shot and they're generally callin' the shots because they have the card. I guess if you get pregnant when you're twelve that's pretty much it.

"The only ones that really get to me are the giant fat sweaty mammas who lay on their cart, sweat running down their face in sheets. This one bitch, when it came time for her to pay the taxable balance, reaches into her shirt, under her bra, underneath her sweaty watermelon titties, and pulls out this flattened wad of folded bills that is literally dripping with sweat. She flicks her hand so that the sweat sprays across the belt and then hands that shit over and I'm supposed to count it! Their breasts arc like the community bank. As soon as they grow tits their shoving money and everything else down there.

"Last Sunday, just after noon ,this boy came in scared to death. He is a regular, lives five houses down the street with his mother and little brother. They are eight or nine. We never see her. The boys come in and buy milk and bread during the week. Well he was terrified, 'Miss JoJo you got to help me! This man is chasing me with a stick!'

"I took him into the booth with me and called his house—no answer of course. Mamma's not home. I took him out to Big Roy [the security guard] and now it was black on black so I just stepped back. Roy scowls down at him and points his big finger and says, 'Boy, you better not be lyin' ta me!'

"The poor kid breaks into tears, 'No, I wouldn't be lyin' ta you, no sir!'

"Then Roy gets the description and it's this dirt bag black panhandler, one of the crazies that run the street and gives everybody shit. The kid accidentally bumped into him and he went off trying to beat him with a stick. Big Roy walked him home and told me he knew the guy, that he was a low life, and that he's going to whoop his ass for going after the kid.

"It's so sad. These kids shouldn't have to raise themselves. They should get some time as children before the world shits all over them."

## Urban Honor by Odd Ways

### Simon, Boost, the White Vice Lords, the Geneva Convention, and Panhandler Taxation

© 2014 James LaFond

I walk by Boost four days a week. Boost suffers from a muscular-skeletal disease that seems to have the same effects as polio. He stands—or leans—up to about 4 feet, and seems to weigh about 70 pounds. Since I have lived in Hamilton he has panhandled in front of the corner pizzeria, managing his wrist-brace crutches and cardboard sign up and down fifty feet of tiered sidewalk. He never begs, always nods with respect to passersby, and seems to have a gleam of intelligence in his brown eyes.

The drug dealers that work that corner have never bothered Boost. He is a civilian, and a handicapped one at that. The Global Islamists and Global Capitalists might ignore every article of the Geneva Convention and murder civilians with impunity—

with some Zionist rabbinical authorities even calling for the death of Islamic babies—but these local thugs abide by a code. In a surreal world where American presidents extol torture, and American senators tell reporters that killing 98 innocent women and children for every suspected Islamist is acceptable military policy, where on earth would one look to find the ancient warrior code of honor upheld?

Boost had been off his corner for a month or so. With his recent return, and the disappearance of Simon, the six-foot four-inch young man who had stolen a pair of crutches and taken over the corner, The Violence Guy sensed a story and homed in, contacting some of his ghetto sources—not wanting to be seen questioning Boost in front of the communication officer of the White Vice Lords, who now claim this corner as part of their drug distribution network.

Here is the short brief story of Simon and Boost, which I cobbled together from two reluctant sources.

Simon walked up to Boost at the end of his shift one night and talked him over into the alley behind the pizzeria where he beat him until he could no longer drag himself. He then informed Boost that the corner was no longer his. The next day Simon took up his stolen crutches [stolen from someone much taller than Boost] and began working the corner under the nose of the cops—who could care less about such things—and beneath the eyes of the White Vice Lords.

The White Vice Lords had recognized Boost as a 'civilian' based on his infirmity and his seniority. Simon, however, took Boost's panhandling spot by force, had committed a crime. Baltimore City Law Enforcement may not care about white guys beating down crippled white guys, but any crime that happens on a drug dealer's corner, and results in an ongoing profit, falls under that drug dealer's jurisdiction.

Now, on such a drug corner crime no longer happens, at least not physically. This corner where bags of dope used to change hands is now just a communications hub. The drug dealers have a vested interest in suppressing gross crime at this location. Indeed, if they could have gotten away with avenging Boost outright without the police locking them up for beating down Simon, I suspect they might have prevented Simon from ever taking that corner.

Simon was taxed an undisclosed fee for working that corner.

Simon, a true dumbass, eventually thought he could get away without paying his thug tax.

Simon is recovering from numerous stab wounds as I write, and Boost is once again working his corner under the benevolent eye of the criminals who decline to tax him, as he is a nonviolent civilian.

Can you name a municipality in the U.S. that does not levee a tax against its citizens, and protects them?

Can you name a military player in our current global war that does not target civilians?

Thank Odin for white-on-white karmicrime.

Junkie Apocalypse

## Celebrating The Panhandler Nation Holiday

© 2014 James LaFond

Big Chev got himself a car. He came in to shop my impeccably stocked yogurt section on Saturday August 30, 2014. That would be yesterday, the morning after my run in with Stretch and Stout, and one day before this, the last day of an overlong month. Before we get to Chev's tale, let us delve into a reality that he 'could give two shits about' which concerns the plight of our Narcostate's favored citizens, its drug addicts.

We might think that addicts have it easy: getting stoned all the time, having not a care in the world, and being supported by the government. It is not all that simple my friends. You see, a drug addict has only five means of earning the income necessary to purchase the drugs that the CIA invested 280 billion dollars in assuring the cultivation of in

Afghanistan—which, is, by the way, the reason the U.S. invaded that nation; not to get the Islamist terrorist, but to prevent the Taliban from continuing to suppress heroin production.

The entire idea behind the Narcostate—as pioneered by the British in China in the 1840s—is to make certain that there is a glut of opiates. The addicts can be counted on to find a means to pay for them. While they are busy with that and the resulting intoxication, they shall be more easily and more profitably managed by their masters.

The junky [Inconsistent spelling is a literary slight. I am therefore very careful when spelling God and the names of others who can kick my ass.] may earn his drug money in one, some or all of the five following ways:

1. Sell his ass and/or mouth to gay sexual predators

2. Panhandle

3. Get injured, sue, and get prescription opiates

4. Get some junkie bitch pregnant, and then kick back as the suddenly transformed ho becomes the pillar of the community; the vector of American Civilization. Then let the baby's mama use the EBT

cash to get her dope and the subsidized baby rent to maintain a crashpad, while he takes the EBT food stamps and sells them for 50 cents on the dollar to pay for his dope. Grandma will feed and pet the resulting rug rat.

5. Actually go out and work for the money by robbing, burglarizing or mugging some less able person, preferably an elderly person.

## Note to Dopefiends

As you can see, there is an expensive and time-consuming downside to 1, 2, 3 and 5. Your most reliable form of income is the 'pension via insemination'. That money comes out between the 6th and the 16th. If you are an above average junky you probably have this budgeted to about 23 days, meaning the last week of the month is unbearable and will kick you into the other methods. Then, 4 times per year [which is why that dude with the funny cap that rents you that efficiency collects weekly rather than monthly rent] there is a fifth week!

"Don dont dah!!!"

Yep, end of your world junky.

Now that you are desperate for drugs you are faced with stiff competition. Here in Harm City 1 of every 10 people is addicted to heroin! Then you have the 1 in 10 who are addicted to booze, and the 1 in 10 who are addicted to all that other stuff. So, when you go out to panhandle you are just one bonerack in a bonerack crash-up derby. What follows are two examples of ineffective attempts to earn drug money, with the first featuring disastrous target selection and the second poor execution.

## Big Chev

"So I'm pulling up here to your wonderful establishment to get my lunch before I head into work. No sooner then I roll up the window some little monkey—couldn't have been older than sixteen—comes up to the window and says, "Do ya gotta dolla?"

"What the fuck is the matter with these people? No 'good morning sir' or 'hi big guy' like the bums used to say back in the day ta stroke you?

"Now apparently every spear-chucker and white stoner in the county assumes that if you have a dollar it belongs to them.

"I look at this person while I'm getting out of the car and he backs of with his mouth hanging open and drool stringing down. I'm looking down at this maggot and he's going, 'Du, du, du, do doo, you gotta dolla?'

"I looked down at him and said, 'Get the fuck away from me head-hunter. Better yet, go spear some other monkey and shrink his head, and I'll give you a dollar for that!'"

I was laughing so hard big Chev said, "You might think it's funny 'cause nobody begs your scrawny ass 'cause you don't have two sticks to rub together. But I'm gettin' sick a this shit."

We wished each other a happy Labor Day and went on our way.

**Yis Fro**

This morning I walked two miles out and down the main drag and back again to stretch my writer's legs. As I walked down the right hand side of the street next to the big crack house that is already back in business after the cops emptied it two weeks back, I looked across the street to the Pakistani drug station. This is a gas station that sells all of the things that stoners need to go with their crack and heroin: cheap knives, Mountain Dew [for the body of your ghetto crack pipe], brass mesh Choreboy pads [for the filter of your ghetto crack pipe], skittles, Arizona tea, Benadryl, cigarettes, flavored cigars used to make blunts, 'spice' synthetic pot, and the indispensable liter in the multipack.

A mixed-race youth with an afro lilting to the left side of his head like Lenny Kravitz playing Einstein in some sci-fi play written by that jerk LaFond, notices me on the deserted 6:38 a.m. Sabbath sidewalk.

The creature managed to stagger over to me across the deserted street. With head nodding, drool stringing, a twitch creeping into his face, he managed to mumble something that might have included a word that approximated cigarette on some other planet. I just walked on by, generally opting for a quick long stride to take me through panhandling zones quickly.

Fifteen minutes later I came back this way, and once again he emerged staggering from the drug station shouting a slurred "Yis! Yiss!" as he limped determinedly into the light traffic yelling with ever more fury for me to slow down and consider the important question he might have one day been able to articulate.

I outpaced him easily and then he saw a young dude lighting a cigarette and began doing the zombie boogie in his direction, only to have the wiry little blonde man shout, "No Pal—stay back."

As I crossed the street I saw a petite black girl with a gigantic posterior that had somehow been jammed into tight white jeans walk down out of the neighborhood behind the crack house and stand with hands on hips at the corner. He eyed her hopefully and before he could even gurgled out his urgent request, she yelled, "Hell no nigga! Get da fuck away. I goin' ta church bitch!"

The man stagger-turned on the center line, lurched toward the drug station, and began to mumble to himself as he sought the more friendly strip of concrete on the east side of the road, pressing his limp afro to the side of his head and staring fixedly at the concrete curb as if it were the Garden of Eden.

EBT cash and stamps begin to come out on the 6th in alphabetical order. That is a long stretch. All of us who have declined to participate in the remote CIA Opium War on America might want to think about how fortunate they are to have whatever it takes to resist the pull of this black hole at the center of our imploding culture.

Stretch and Stout

**Panhandling and Managing Your Approach Zone**

© 2014 James LaFond

This past Friday night at about 11 p.m. I woke up from my seat on the bus as my head bobbled to a stop—my stop. I hurried off the bus, put on my pack and checked the time on my phone. As always it is my instinct, even when half awake, to step away from others; to always and forever put distance between me and the diseased masses of human excretia. My paranoid mind wakes and nods off to sleep in a Hobbesian world, a rundown town that H. L. Mencken once describes as 'the ruins of a once great medieval city.'

As the bus pulled off the boy I offloaded with was walking off up the street and two innocent unarmed black teens were eyeballing me from the shelter across the street. The first helpless child stood six five and went about 170. The second helpless child

153

stood five six and went about 130, with a very muscular frame. I shall name them Stretch and Stout.

I decided not to connect with the bus that would be pulling up to that shelter in 10 minutes, and stepped of left, farther away from them and checked the time again, before crossing the street thirty feet to their right.

Stretch walked across the street toward me. When he saw me look at his feet and not look up, he asked as I pocketed my phone, "Excuse me sir. You have a light?"

These kids were probably just out having a good semi-adult time without much money as their mamma's EBT cash and stamps ran out at least two weeks ago. They had probably bummed a cig and just wanted a light. But, I could have been being measured for a mugging.

I shook my head 'no' without looking up and walked across the street. Stretch was streetwise enough to know that I was streetwise, and that I was not the friendly type, so he just backed off, at all times maintaining a safe distance of about 10 feet. At night, on the street—and we literally were in the middle of a fairly busy street—a person with any survival sense has an expanded sense of his or her 'personal space'.

As I walked across and Stretch back-walked parallel to me to the shelter without closing distance Stout began shouting—obviously with a few drinks under his adolescent belt:

"Yo got a ticket?"

"Yo, yo, yo got a ticket?"

"Yo, yo done wit yo ticket!?"

"Yo, I'm talkin' ta yo muthafuca!"

"Whachyo disrospectin' fo yo?"

"Ged bag 'ere when I talkin' ta yo!"

I was now 20 feet beyond and 5 feet to my right from him, walking across a dark parking lot of a closed store, where some dude was sitting on a curb smoking pot. I could hear Stout coming around the corner from the stop over the gravel and dirt. I slid my right hand under my pack into the back pocket of my shorts and palmed the razor that was there and slid the hand back up into my front pocket. I never looked back as that is a fearful act that encourages pursuit.

I was now more concerned with whoever might be in the shadowed wall spaces of the lot. Stout was going to touch me and get his wrist slashed. In my mind he was already being taken care of by the autorazor. Stretch knew what the hell he was about. If he was part of this, he was the more dangerous of the two. And then there was the possibility that the pot smoker was with them, and what the shadows might hold as well.

Then, as Stout's brand new athletic wear slapped the asphalt of the lot I heard Stretch say quietly, "Let him go."

Stout continued to come on and Stretch raised his voice and said with more resolve, in a commanding tone, "Don't follow that man."

Stout obeyed, and screamed venomously into the night at my back, "Bitch!"

In my opinion Stretch and Stout were just two kids that had scraped together enough change to share a half pint of rum, had bummed a cigarette and were loathe to let their night of adventure go just yet and wanted to hangout some more. These innocent unarmed black teens were engaged in the venerable urban tradition of 'doing stupid shit'.

I do not believe that these guys were trying to set me up. I think this was a case of escalated panhandling. Many bus patrons willingly give away their bus ticket at the end of the night. Indeed, it is such a common practice among people at this transfer point that these boys were well within reason if they had simply spent their bus money on booze and were counting on getting home through a charitable donation of a used bus ticket on the part of some other poor person who cared.

Unfortunately, there was no one present who cared.

I think that Stout just became emotionally hurt when I refused to 'respect' him. Apparently Stretch has seen enough to know that there is great risk to any lone man who shows too much respect to strangers in the night and had the presence of mind to talk Stout from his collision course with a stranger with a hand in a pocket in the dark.

The 7 Panhandler Nations

**Adaptable Faces of Urban Blight**

© 2014 James LaFond

This is a primer on the seven panhandling archetypes identified by 'The Violence Guy' in his twenty years documenting the social sewer of Baltimore Maryland. Sketches of real panhandlers who clearly fit a single type will be used instead of generic templates. Generic and panhandler ought not to be used in the same sentence.

## 1. The Beggar

The panhandler who stakes out one location and cultivates an image of tolerable passivity is as old as civilization. Old Bill is a barely functional alcoholic who lives in his sister's basement and manages to get dressed and to the concrete median strip at the underpass five days per week. Bill and those like him are on the urban endangered species list, being pushed to the margins by the two evolved forms of the stationary panhandler below.

## 2. Apex Panhandler

Marc was a violent homeless alcoholic. In the mid 1990s he found a $300 per day white guilt corner in front of Golden Ring Mall on U.S. Route #7 at the I-95 ramp. He followed the panhandler who was working the corner down into the overgrown gully where he relived himself, beat the shit out of him, 'left him lay' and appropriated the sign [the corner being a package deal], returning to the guilt-ridden world above with a salesman's smile on his dark face. My coworker Stick [who was not called Stick for his lack of body fat], who had once beat Marc in a street fight, seriously considered quitting his job and taking on Marc, but went into prostitution instead.

## 3. Communal Panhandler

Little John was a heroin addict, a junkie. He lived in house with five other junkies. They had 1 car, a busted up old Chevette. This car was only used for earning money as a gypsy cab. While one house member operated the car another worked the corner at the Hyatt Regency on Light Street. The house members changed shifts, but that sign never rested. John and his five roommates made enough to pay their $1,100 monthly rent, stay well, and buy cigarettes by the case. Communal panhandlers are an obvious evolutionary adaptation of the beggar banding together to defend against the apex panhandler.

### 4. The Bum

Smitty used to sleep with his legs in the storm drain under the sidewalk, his chest in the gutter, and his face on the warm asphalt heated by the steam that billowed up from the bowels of the rat infested Federal Hill sewers, behind the bagel shop. He was a thirty-something alcoholic who would mumble for change when I stepped over his body. Guys like this usually have an income and just beg so they have an excuse to loiter where they fell down drunk. Smitty was on disability and received an SSI check, which was mailed to his brother's address. This is the guy sleeping on the steam grate who generally puts little effort into begging, but seems to do it more on principal. He is close to a classic hobo or resourceful homeless person, but lacks the self respect to stop begging.

## 5. The Artist

Ransome dressed in gold slacks and silk shirts to go panhandling. He would work the Inner Harbor area as a tourist who claimed he had been robbed, ripped off, or ditched by his tour group. He would ask for cab fair to the hotel which would run about $5. The man should have been working in Hollywood and was a joy to listen to. Other artists might offer themselves as a guide, a bodyguard or a porter, the offer to 'work for food' having been so overused by the beggars that it is no longer viable. They are generally mobile and sometimes use automobiles which they pretend are broken down or out of gas in order to illicit sympathy. Pregnant women and panhandlers with babies fall on the fringes of this large creative category.

## 6. The Shark

Brill Cream was a big hulking man who walked with a hunched back and rolled shoulders, scowling out from under his heavy brows—the Bluto of panhandlers. He would ask for 'change' or 'a dollar', rewarding the generous with his absence and afflicting the stingy with his presence. He would on occasion escalate to strong arm robbery or extortion.

## 7. The Minnow

Denise is a crack addict who was doing okay until her boyfriend got sent to prison. She soon found herself homeless, and for the last three years has been living in the interior doorway of a friend's apartment. The outer door is broken and blows open at night. She can only stay there after dark and spends all day walking the streets scrounging for change on the ground, un-cashed lottery tickets, usable bus tickets that can be sold, and begging for a quarter. If you have a quarter she will ask for fifty cents.

She will also bum a cigarette and then sell it for a quarter, usually contenting herself with smoking used gutter scrounged cigarettes. One of her strategies is to politely lurk around the break area outside of a supermarket and offer to take a half finished cigarette from an employee who gets called back in before their smoke is done.

The slim rewards enjoyed by female panhandlers like Denise point to the implicit threat that male panhandlers pose. Female panhandlers who do not partner with a man or work as part of a commune do not last long, and soon turn to dumpster diving and other means of eking an income from the streets.